*"The food here is terrible, and the portions are too small."*

WOODY ALLEN

*The Dubliner 100 Best Restaurants 2008*
Edited by TREVOR WHITE
Photography by KLAUDYNA KARCZEWSKA
Design by SIMON O'CONNOR

First edition, published November 2007

ISBN 0-9542188-6-8

Published by *The Dubliner* Magazine,
23 Wicklow Street, Dublin 2, Ireland.
T: (3531) 635 9822. E: editor@thedubliner.ie.
W: www.thedubliner.ie

# The Dubliner

# 100 BEST RESTAURANTS

EDITED BY TREVOR WHITE

*Nonna Valentina*

# FOREWORD

Santa Rita is delighted to collaborate with *The Dubliner* on this definitive directory of the capital's 100 Best Restaurants for the sixth consecutive year. There have been many changes in those six years. Restaurants have come and gone, tastes have developed, and this year's book is a snapshot of an evolving culinary landscape.

Santa Rita was founded on change. Don Domingo Fernandez brought in some of the finest French vine stocks to begin a new, rich wine tradition. During the Chilean struggle for Independence, Bernardo O'Higgins, along with 120 of his followers, took refuge from Spanish troops in Santa Rita's cellars.

As tastes change and a young generation of Irish chefs begin a new era for Dublin restaurants, Santa Rita remains as innovative and popular as ever. There are many new dining experiences to be discovered in these pages. Might I suggest that each time you toast a great meal, you do so with a glass of Santa Rita?

JOE QUINSEY
*General Manager*
*Gilbeys of Ireland*

# INTRODUCTION

Where shall we go for dinner tonight? When this question is asked in Raheny, Rathfarnham or Ranelagh, the answer is usually short. Most of us have our favourites, and even the greatest menu tart often returns to the same three or four places. This book introduces the reader to a variety of new kitchens. A few, at least, will leave you satiated, happy, not much poorer – it's an insurance policy for the stomach.

We are creatures of habit, yet it's also true that we have never had so much choice. There are now over 1,000 restaurants in Dublin. Initially, all attract a flurry of interest, maybe even hype. But the vast majority will struggle to survive.

If you believe the prophets of doom – David McWilliams comes to mind – the Irish economy is due a sharp downturn. If that happens, we will suddenly become a lot more discriminating about where we spend our money. And a lot of new restaurants will go to the wall. It's hard to feel sorry for *all* of them.

Smart restaurateurs are now consolidating, reimagining where necessary, preparing for a different economic climate. They will survive, not least because they are already familiar with a new cultural reality: the diner has become the critic. The might of the web now enables everyone to bite back, and the better operators have already upped their game in response.

All this is, in a way, good news for consumers, who have never been so powerful. And fine dining, once the preserve of a privileged few, is now more accessible than ever. We're lucky to live in such a time of plenty, and there is a moral obligation to extract what pleasure we can from life. (There is nothing smug or impractical about this sentiment. Pleasure begets pleasure.)

So take your usual table. Or discover the gem that has just opened up around the corner. In fact, why not open this book at random and vow to inspect the result? When you get there, give thanks to providence, and raise a glass to Irish economists.

May they *never* get it right!

TREVOR WHITE
*The Dubliner*

# NORTHSIDE RULES!

*Chapter One*

Thousands of Dubliners voted in our annual poll to find the city's most popular restaurant. For the second time in three years, Chapter One was the winner of the Santa Rita People's Choice Award. When it opened, 16 years ago, many people thought Martin Corbett and head chef Ross Lewis were mad; Parnell Square was a culinary wilderness. Today C1 is as popular among local bigwigs – Michael Colgan and Aengus Fanning are regulars – as it is among Dublin's foodies. It has just reopened after the cunning addition of a dining room that is flooded with natural light. Alas this means that capacity has decreased... making it even harder to get a reservation! If all else fails, tell them *The Dubliner* sent you.

*Santa Rita*

PEOPLE'S CHOICE AWARD 2008

# ALEXIS

*French Flair*

Joan Collins in *Dynasty*? No. Alexis honours Alexis Benoit Soyer, the French chef who established the first soup kitchen during the Famine. This modern incarnation is the brainchild of Alan O'Reilly, formerly of Clarets and Morels, and his brother Patrick. The room is large and unadorned, like a canteen – in deference to Soyer's original premises perhaps. As for the food – impeccable ingredients, cooked with flair and well presented. Go on a weekday rather than a Sunday – the daily menus feature delights like roast wood pigeon tartlet and braised beef ribs with a sauce conceived by the great man himself. Simple but substantial brasserie food is what Dublin needs. Alexis delivers.

*17-18 Patrick Street, Dun Laoghaire, County Dublin. 280 8872*

# ANDERSONS

*Glasnevin Gold*

An out of the way posh-nosh retreat in Glasnevin? Where? Well, it's only hidden to us outsiders: locals know all about Andersons, a continental-style café and food hall in an old butcher's shop. It's usually packed, so be prepared to wait a while. Try to nab a seat outside – we're not crazy about the rather lifeless back room. Order one of the special platters: we like the Mediterranean selection of ham, salami, mortadella, vegetables, Italian cheese and fresh bread (€14.95). There are almost 200 wines on offer, and corkage is just €6. Food and wine is available to take away too. Bring some to feed the squirrels in the nearby Botanic Gardens, a pastoral haven in this city of cranes.

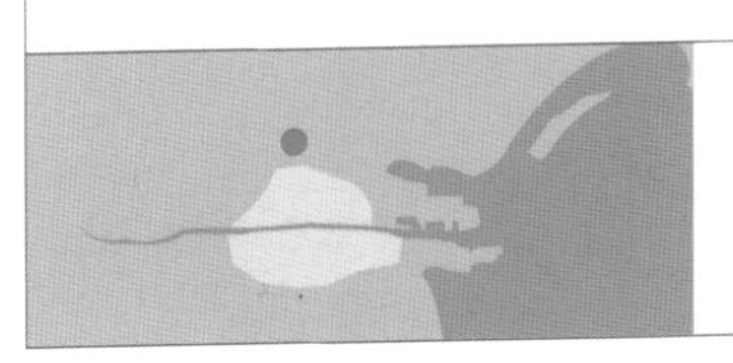

*3 The Rise, Glasnevin,*
*Dublin 9. 837 8394.*
*www.andersons.ie*

# AQUA

*Hunky John Dory*

The erstwhile home of Howth Yacht Club, Aqua's USP is a fine view over the sea towards Malahide. The decor is modern with a nautical touch – white linen, clean lines, floor-to-ceiling windows, pictures of local landscapes. Head chef Tom Walsh uses locally-sourced ingredients and presents simple, thoughtful dishes. The menu includes rabbit, venison, duck and Irish beef dishes, but you'll never throw back the fish. Get the oysters with red onion (€12.50) followed by sea-scallops, bell pepper and fennel stew (€34) or lobster with foie gras (€46). Follow up with a glass of Chateau La Bouade Sauternes (€7.50) and tarte tatin (€7.95). The a la carte menu adds up: go for the early bird, followed by a stroll along the pier.

*1 West Pier, Howth,*
*County Dublin.*
*832 0690.*
*www.aqua.ie*

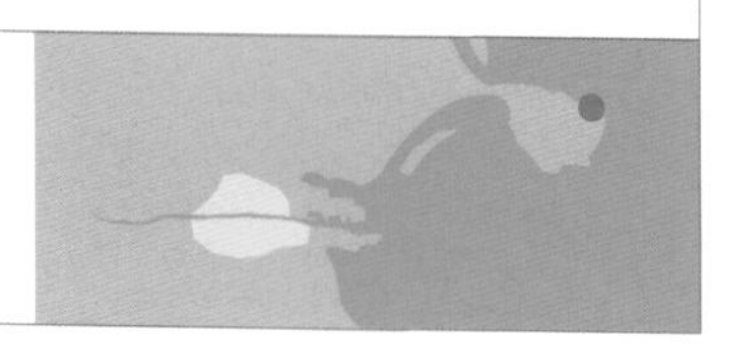

# AVOCA

*On High*

Six years on, Dublin's best in-store café remains one of the most popular lunch destinations in the city centre. The 100-seater dining room is usually full of Southside mums, exhausted from all that trekking around downstairs, a miscellany of cool local design and exotic *tchotchkes*. Head chef John Dunne trained with Raymond Blanc, whose ambitious motto, "The good does not interest us; the sublime does," is somewhat reflected in his protégé's menu: wholesome fare like fish pie with baby leaves (€13.95) and Parma-wrapped chicken with ricotta and spinach stuffing (€11.95). Michael Stipe and Daniel Day Lewis are fans. For those on the run, there are good salad-bar options in the basement.

*11-13 Suffolk Street,*
*Dublin 2.*
*677 4215.*
*www.avoca.ie*

# BANG

*Tasty Twins*

Christian and Simon Stokes originally intended Bang to be a café bar – a little brother to the Unicorn, which is co-owned by their father, Jeff. Dublin's glitterati soon flocked to the stylish, minimalist space, attracted by the staff – hot! – and Lorcan Cribben's cooking. Try his tangy white crab salad (€9.25). Follow it with beef medallions with shallots, mushrooms and Béarnaise (€28.50). The best way to enjoy Bang is to make a night of it, cocktails and all. You may not *love* the food, but you have to admire the initiative of the Stokes twins. An outdoor terrace should be in operation by Summer 2008, and even the dogs on the street (Afghan Hounds?) are talking about their new club on Stephen's Green.

*11 Merrion Row, Dublin 2.*
*676 0898.*
*www.bangrestaurant.com*

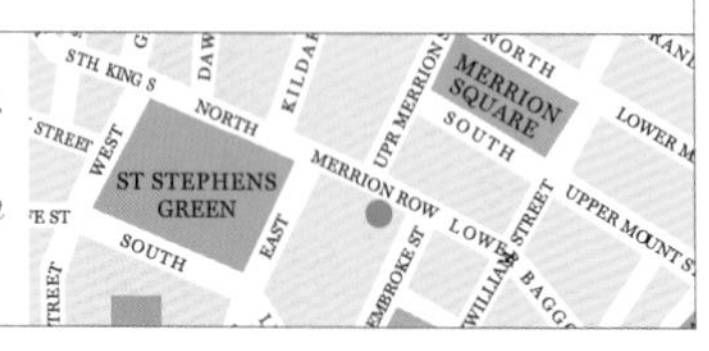

# BAR ITALIA

*Best Buzz*

An old favourite. The all-Italian staff is warm and generous and the food is consistently good. This is part of the domain of Stefano Crescenzi and Davide Izzo, the team behind Dunne & Crescenzi and Nonna Valentina. We love the cheap-as-chips minestrone soup (€4.90) and the antipasti misti (€8.50). And if there's homemade gnocchi on the specials list, risk a scalding and grab it with both hands. Wonderful coffee. The small dining room has a comforting Italian feel: lots of yelling, clanging and hand gestures. On a nice day, sit outside. There's a sister branch in Mick Wallace's Italian Quarter across the Quays – it's slightly more formal, but the food is equally good and the wine selection is better.

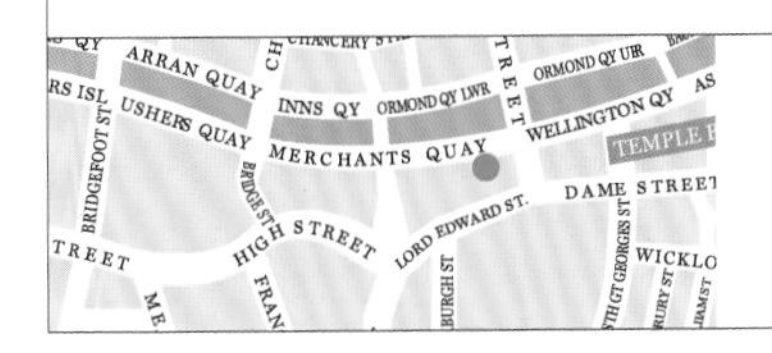


*26 Lower Ormond Quay, Dublin 8.*
*874 1000.*
*www.baritalia.ie*

# BIJOU

*French in D6*

The finest (only?) French restaurant in Rathgar is divided into a more formal upstairs dining room, where booking is a must, and an equally good but less fussy ground-floor bistro. On high, there's soft lighting, velvet seats and a welcoming fire. Start with the pan-fried scallops (€13.95), follow up with roast breast of Challans duck (€27.50). There's a romantic outside terrace (read: smoking area) up there too. Down below, the comfy banquettes cry out to hungover lawyers on a Saturday afternoon. The menu is simple and comforting: fishcakes with coconut (€9.95), Hicks jumbo sausages (€13.50), rib-eye steak (€19.95), homemade cod and chips (€15.95). They also serve a mean Bloody Mary. Live a little!

*47 Highfield Road,*
*Rathgar, Dublin 6.*
*496 1518*

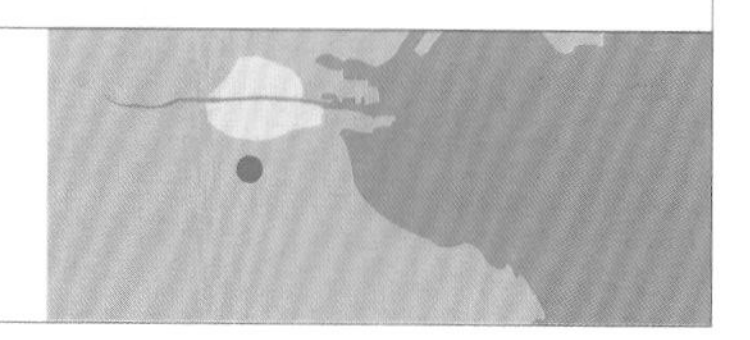

# BÓBÓ'S

*Holy Cow!*

Ireland has finally embraced the gourmet burger trend. Bóbó's, brought to us courtesy of Jay Bourke, was first out of the stocks. At the weekend, the cow-hide benches are packed with 20-somethings looking for something more than a battered sausage from Roma II and drunken countrymen gazing incredulously at the chips' €3.95 price tag. It's more dignified on a weeknight – the staff are friendly, the burgers sit happily on the fence between juicy and charred. Compared to rival Jo Burger, the toppings here are classic and safe: we like the "Danny" – Cashel blue, cream cheese, tomato, rocket and "Special Sauce" (€7.95). Save room for an ice-cream float (€3.55). Way better than your average chipper.

*22 Wexford Street,*
*Dublin 2.*
*400 5750.*
*www.bobos.ie*

# BON APPETIT

*Michelin Man*

Dubliners love to speculate about who's going to get the next Michelin star. The smart money, it seems, is divided between two restaurants in which chef Oliver Dunne has played a part: Mint in Ranelagh, which he left in 2006, and his new place, Bon Appetit in Malahide. Our money is on the latter, where the cooking is assured, and the decor – silken walls, crisp linen, chandeliers – is plush. Note: this is not a French restaurant. Dunne's style is modern, with a light touch and an emphasis on presentation. Try to keep your credit card above water, especially if you're trying the tasting menus. Save some money on the trip home: if you book a table for no later than 8pm, it's just about possible to catch the last DART.

*9 James Terrace,
Malahide, County
Dublin. 845 0314.
www.bonappetit.ie*

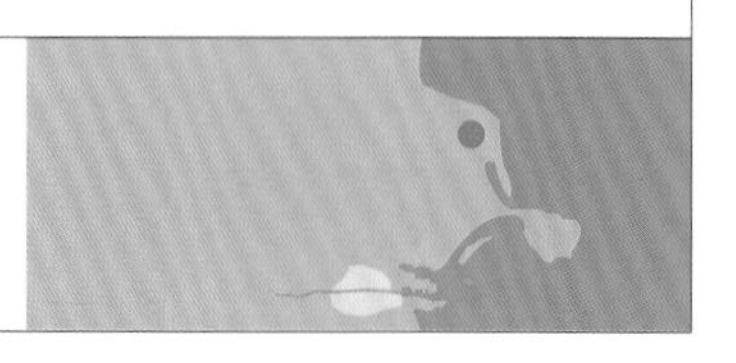

# BRASSERIE SIXTY6

*New York Lunch*

This self-proclaimed "stylish, busy, noisy restaurant" has really upped its game in the two years since it opened its doors. Those put off by the shaky service in the first few weeks have come back on board, the prices are reasonable and the food has always been tasty: our dinner favourites are the sausage and mash (€13.95), rotisserie chicken (€14.75) and New York meatloaf (€15.50). Plenty of veggie options too – try the lentil, bean and sweetcorn cake (€12). For a true feast – beware of the meat sweats – you can pre-order a suckling pig with veg and spuds for a table of ten (€345). Sixty6 is taking brunch customers from nearby Odessa at the weekend too – most come for the open skillet full breakfast (€10.95).

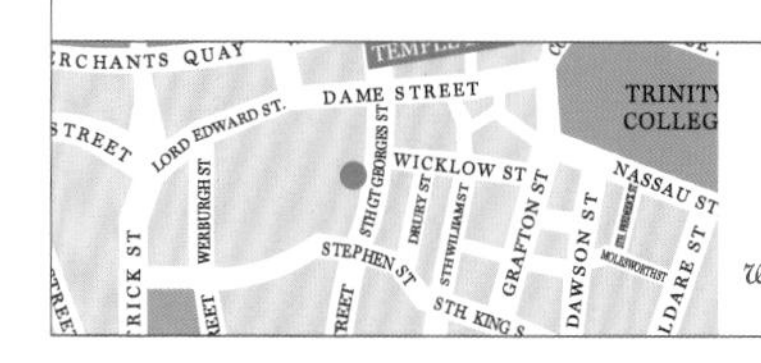


*66 South Great George's Street, Dublin 2.*
*400 5878.*
*www.brasseriesixty6.com*

# BROWNES BRASSERIE

*Boutique Beauty*

This handsome little hotel and restaurant was eaten up by the corporate world when it joined the Stein hotel chain in 2003. The arrival of Aussie executive chef David Willcocks and a recent redecoration both illustrate good intentions. Service is relaxed and unobtrusive considering the old school surroundings. You may have to skip the wine if you're on a budget – house bottles start at €35.50 – but the food is relatively good value. The menu is small but classic: we ate crispy fried braised pork cheek with potato purée (€13.95) followed by chargrilled sea bream (€25.50), both delicious. We love that chunky chips are called "pommes Pont Neuf" – think you're the only posh one around here, Lord Shelbourne?

*22 St Stephen's Green,*
*Dublin 2.*
*638 3939.*
*www.brownesdublin.com*

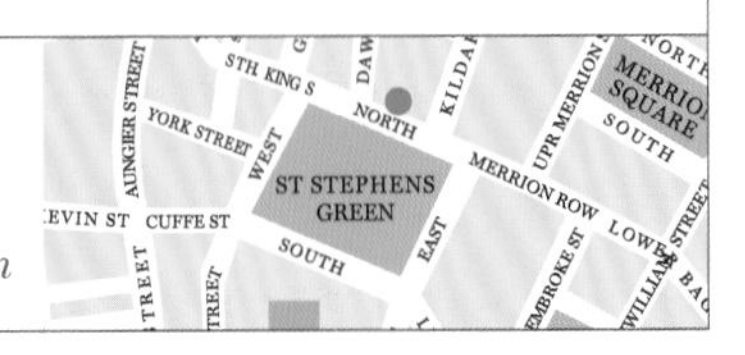

Intelligent Life
on the web?

---

*Read the
Dubliner blog.*

# BYBLOS

*Cheap Lebanese*

Hassan Assaf owns the only Irish pub in Beirut, Paddy's Bar. It's been closed for the last year due to the troubles, but it seems that Beirut's loss is Dublin's gain. After buying the lease of a mediocre Italian off Wicklow Street, Hassan gave it a makeover – with the help of his father Mustafa, who did the beautiful, and rather *flaithiúlach*, marble and stonework – and opened a Lebanese mezze house named after the oldest city in the world. The food is fresh and inexpensive: we love the mezze tasting platters (from €25). Service is cheerful and plenty of the customers are Lebanese, which is a good sign. Perfect for mid-week lunch, or to watch a woman do mad things with her belly at the weekend.

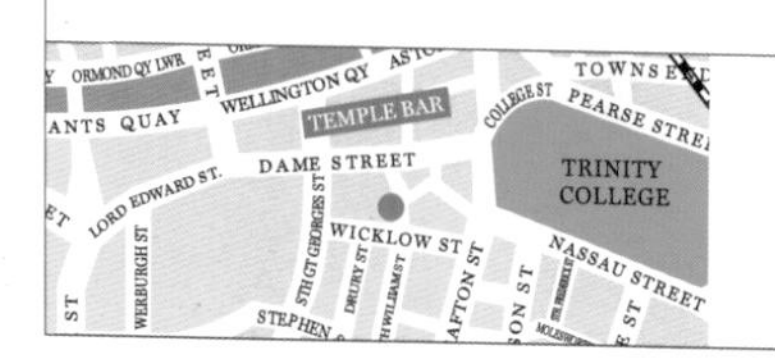


*11 St Andrew's Street,*
*Dublin 2.*
*679 1517*

# CAFÉBARDELI

*No Fuss*

Bewley's on Grafton Street is a national treasure. Dublin's biggest restaurant – there are 350 seats – is now managed by Jay Bourke. With CafeBarDeli, he has struck on a winning formula: reasonably-priced, simple, Mediterranean-inspired food in a huddled, city-centre environment with friendly staff. No muss, no fuss. Tourists come for tea and scones, hungry shoppers for lunch and at night, young urbanites for bites, wine and people-watching. The menu hasn't changed much since the first CBD opened in 2001. Go with a big group: start with antipasti (€11.50 each), then split pizzas (€12-€15) and salads (around €10 for a large) and many bottles of mouth-tingling Fat Bastard chardonnay.

*78/79 Grafton Street,*
*Dublin 2.*
*672 7720.*
*www.cafebardeli.ie*

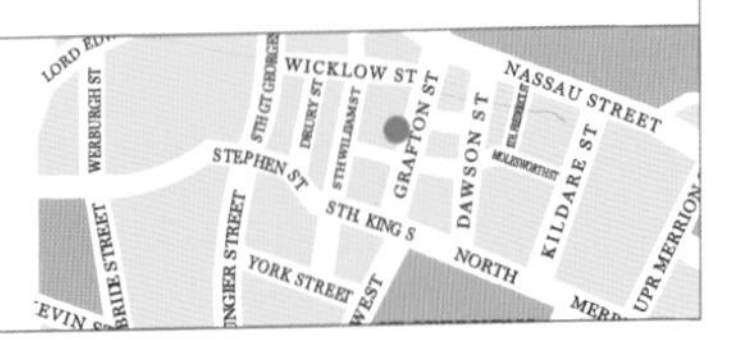

# CAFÉ FRESH

*Veggie Goodness*

If 90% of the customers in a vegetarian restaurant are meat-eaters, it must be doing something right. Mary Farrell – who also owns Fresh deli on Leeson Street – has created a menu that doesn't just leave out the meat, but includes organic, seasonal ingredients, with none of the grassy/cardboard nightmares you often get in vegetarian places. You'll see as many local workers in here looking for a tasty lunch alternative as hippies questioning the provenance of the organic beetroot. On our last visit we had a scrumptious fennel, mushroom and potato gratin with Drumlin smoked cheese (€8.95). Grab one of the tables overlooking the shopping centre and watch the (retail) world go by.

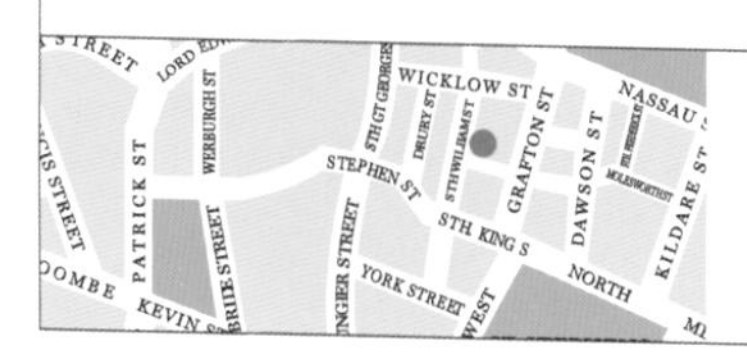


*Powerscourt Centre,*
*South William Street,*
*Dublin 2. 671 9669.*
*www.cafe-fresh.com*

# THE CAKE CAFÉ

*What A Treat!*

Where the heck is this place? Everyone has heard of Michelle Darmody's little hotspot, but is it a left before Whelan's or a... Tucked into the courtyard of the eco-friendly Daintree Apartments, this lunch-only café is as tranquil as it is hidden. Mismatched crockery and flowery prints lend kitsch charm and the staff are friendly. The menu is simple: tarts, salads, terrines and sandwiches – all organic, local and super-fresh. It takes confidence in the quality of your ingredients to serve unadorned sardines on toast. And the cakes? The dense chocolate gateau would stop bullets and every crumb of pastry is rich with buttery goodness. Drool. Open until 8pm, closed Sundays.

*The Daintree Building,*
*Pleasants Place, Dublin 2.*
*478 9394.*
*www.thecakecafé.ie*

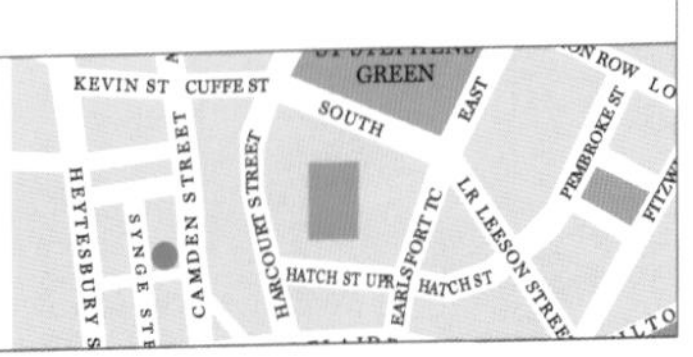

# CANAL BANK CAFÉ

*Starry Local*

This quirky neighbourhood restaurant – it's *not* a café – was formerly known as Dish and is still owned by Trevor Browne. It's a popular spot for weekend brunch: expect comfort foods, and in proper portions. One might have burgers (from €11.95), steak sandwiches (€13.95), Brooklyn meatloaf (€17.50, recommended) or fish and chips (€17.95), along with massive sides of onion rings (€4.95) and buttered spinach (€4.25). Note to gluttonous slobs: they make their own lemon curd and vanilla ice cream. Decent wine list, too, with a wide selection under €30. The restaurant itself is airy and comfortable – avoid the window seats – and the staff are relaxed and helpful. Child-friendly. P.S. Beware of the minor celebrities.

*146 Upper Leeson Street,*
*Dublin 4.*
*664 2135.*
*www.canalbankcafé.com*

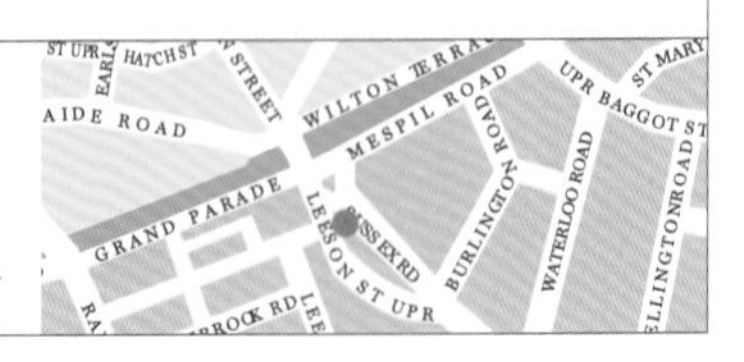

# CAVISTONS

*Spiffing Seafood*

Monkstown mummies often queue out the door of Cavistons food emporium, which sells fish, meat, cheese, veg and gourmet foods. In 1996, the family opened a restaurant next door, bringing in Noel Cusack as head chef. It's tiny, only seating 28, and it's just open for lunch, so reserve well in advance. There are three sittings: go for the last one at 3pm, sit back and savour a bottle of wine with the freshest fish in Dublin. If you don't fancy the daily special, have chargrilled swordfish with mango and melon (€26). Most plates come with boiled spuds and salad on the side. The menu is literally fish-only, so call ahead with special requests. P.S. Owner Peter Caviston is slightly barmy.

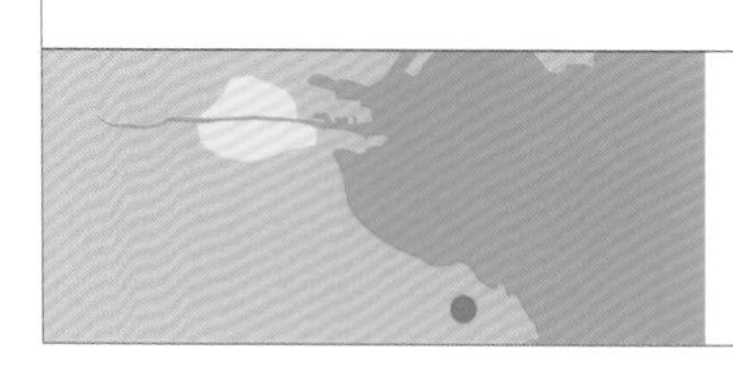

*59 Glasthule Road, Sandycove, County Dublin. 280 9120. www.cavistons.com*

# CHAPTERHOUSE CAFÉ

*Next Best Thing*

Chapter One is booked up until early in the 23rd Century. However, it is still posssible to eat Ross Lewis' food – has been possible, in fact, for the last 16 years – in this cheapish canteen upstairs, at the back of the Dublin Writers Museum. It's not easy to find but the museum itself is well worth exploring anyway. A large blackboard menu lends an old school-house feel, along with the bread-baskets on the glass counter and wooden trays. Busy! Have something simple like a turnip soup (€3.65) and homemade bread and butter, or one of the €9 hot specials – meatloaf and spaghetti with tomato sauce. The specials and roasts change daily and there is a lovely outside seating area.

*Dublin Writers Museum, 18 Parnell Square, Dublin 1. 872 2077. www.writersmuseum.com*

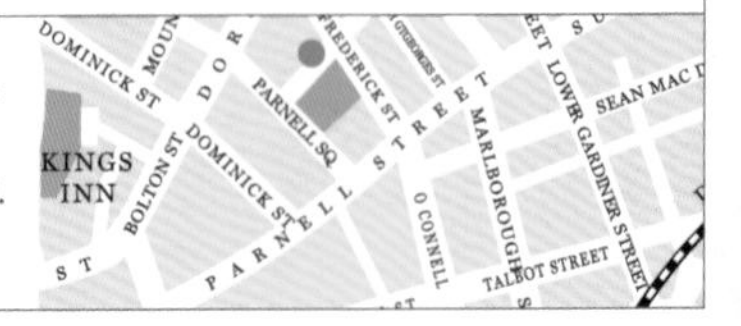

CHAPTERHOUSE CAFE

# CHAPTER ONE

*We Want In!*

A slightly over-celebrated classic? We say this out of frustration: C1 is always full. Ross Lewis and Martin Corbett kept the original features of the Georgian vaults – old brickwork, sash windows, fine art – and added modern touches – earth-toned furniture, crisp white tablecloths – to create a handsome basement restaurant. Try the quail with wilted greens, ham and girolle mushrooms (€16). The charcuterie trolley (€20) is out of this world. The taster menu (€70 per head) is well worth it. Wonderful service, led by the peerless Declan Maxwell, and a stunning wine list. Finally, this is Michael Colgan country: Martin Sheen, Al Pacino and Barbra Streisand were in last summer.

*18/19 Parnell Square, Dublin 1.*
*873 2266. www.chapter onerestaurant.com*

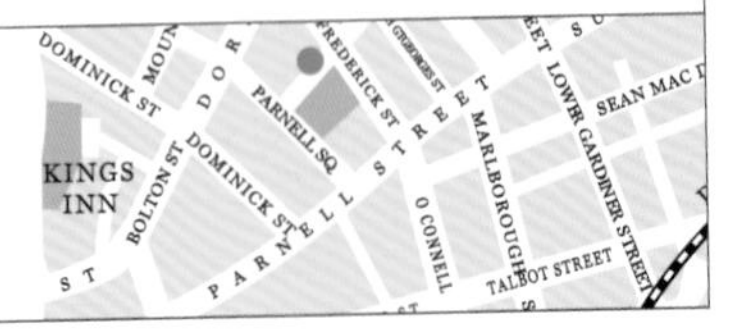

# THE CHEESE PANTRY

*Lazy Lunch*

The Cheese Pantry is housed in what was once a fantastic butcher's shop called Youkstetter's on the Drumcondra Road. Shame the butcher's has gone but what a welcome reincarnation. The dining room is tiny, but bright and airy. We ordered the Lazy Lunch Platter for two (€17.95). It was brought out by someone who we presumed to be the owner, such was his passion for the food we had ordered. The large platter held generous portions of Gubbeen, venison salami, crozier cheese, cornichons, smoked salmon and other palate-pleasers. Plenty of tasty produce to take home too. Ask about "the greatest olive oil on earth" – we think it just might be.

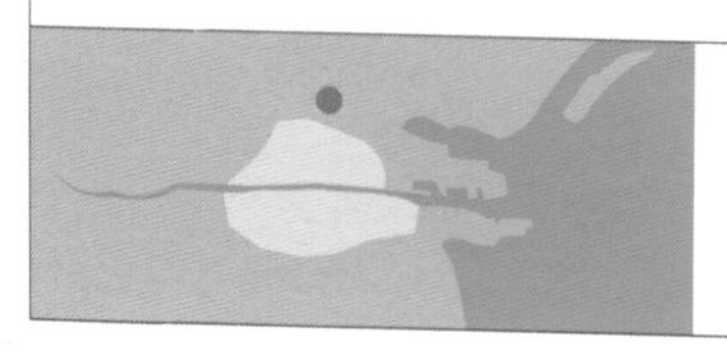

*104 Drumcondra Road Upper, Drumcondra, Dublin 9. 857 2088*

# CHEZ MAX

*'Allo 'Allo*

This French bistro lurks under the walls of Dublin Castle. Well, it's not actually a French bistro, more a mind's eye recreation: pastis jugs, arty posters... Kind of like *'Allo 'Allo.* The big disappointment is that nobody says, "Leeesen carefulleee, I will say thees ernly wernce." Max, the boss, sits outside smoking Gauloises, clad in leather like a weekend biker or a successful 'mec.' The food is mainstream French, very good and reasonably priced. The menu has been purged of what the Irish consider "unpleasantries" – *cuisses de grenouilles* – but you'll still find a dinky French onion soup (€5.90), delicious *boeuf bourguignon* (€15) and a waist-expanding pork belly with cheese and garlic mash (€14.50).

*1 Palace Street, Dublin 2.*
*633 7215*

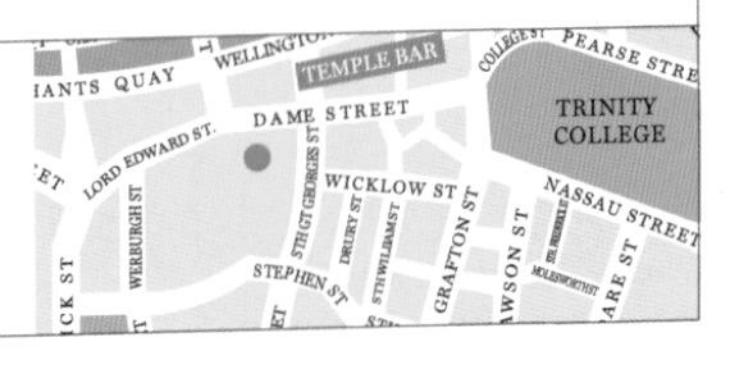

# THE CHILI CLUB

*Discreet Thai*

First impressions are not encouraging: there's the name, the slightly-dodgy-alley location, and the wary looks on arrival. The interior of the tiny dining room – bland cream – is livened up by artwork and decorations in gentle green and gold. The food hasn't (really) been tamed for Irish tastes. Sharing a platter, I bartered away my share of the prawns for more satay chicken. For mains, the *plar nung see yu* was particularly good. Pricey enough at dinner. Best at lunch, alone, with a newspaper. Not the sort of place in which one celebrates a birthday. The dining room is too small for public displays of drunkenness. (This, by the way, was the first Thai restaurant Dublin ever had.)

*1 Anne's Lane, South Anne Street, Dublin 2.*
*677 3721*

# CORNUCOPIA

*Veggies Unite*

Deirdre McCafferty started a health food store and café with her late husband Neil in 1986. Neil was the original chef, making fresh hummous, tabouleh, curries and soups in the back. The food was so popular that they created this "life-enhancing" vegetarian restaurant. Plans are now afoot to double its size by taking over the bag shop next door. It's a welcome find for anyone on a vegetarian, gluten-free, yeast-free, low fat or vegan diet. Excellent array of curries, bakes, pasta dishes, casseroles and pies, many with an Eastern influence. The veggie breakfast was last year voted one of *The Dubliner*'s top ten meals under €10. Funky staff, fascinating diners, much opportunity for impromptu conversation. We like.

*19 Wicklow Street,*
*Dublin 2.*
*677 7583.*
*www.cornucopia.ie*

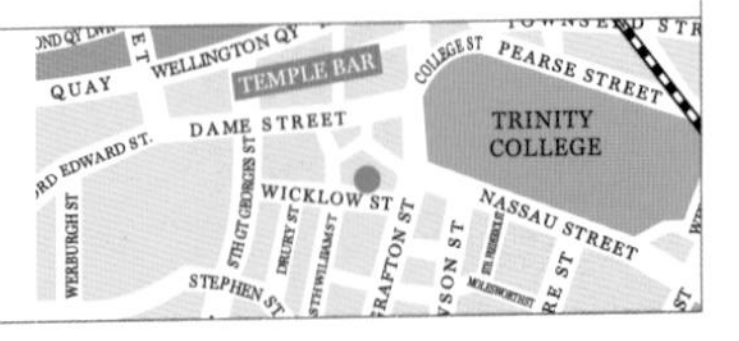

# DALI'S

*Honest Southsider*

There's nothing surreal or particularly Spanish about this place. Maybe it was Dali's dictum that inspired the owners: "Drawing is the honesty of the art. There is no possibility of cheating. It is either good or bad." The food here is, honestly, good: European and Asian fare, with an emphasis on locally-caught seafood and interesting accompaniments. One might have organic salmon carpaccio with ruby grapefruit, shaved fennel, red onion and limoncello (€12), a strong, tangy opener. Follow with rack of lamb with broccoli and mascarpone crust, olive and oregano mash and mint chutney (€28). The prices are high for a suburban joint, and with few wines below the €30 mark (and many far above) it all adds up.

*63/65 Main Street, Blackrock, County Dublin. 278 0660. www.dalis.ie*

# DARWIN'S

*Steaks Plus*

More than a steakhouse? Yes and no. The atmosphere is a little sterile in the Aungier Street home of "evolutionary food" – tables too close together, canteen vibe – but you can't argue with the food. Standout starters include a wild mushroom risotto (€9) and scallops with confit of fennel, mizuna salad, lemon and orange dressing (€12). Among the steaks, our favourite is the succulent premium eye fillet (€29) with a choice of pepper cream or mushroom sauce, garlic butter, Béarnaise or red wine jus. A cheerful waiter will suggest side orders of onion rings, garlic mushrooms and house chips – at €4 each, they're all winners. Separate vegetarian menu – one might have the couscous cake and stuffed red peppers (€18).

*16 Aungier Street,*
*Dublin 2.*
*475 7511*

# DAX

*Cosy Basement*

Celebrity, socialite, businessman or bus driver - everyone gets a warm welcome in Olivier Meisonnave's Georgian basement wine bar and restaurant. It's a great spot for business meetings, lunch or casual drinks: well-spaced tables mean you can munch and chat away in relative peace. At night the calm, dimly-lit space is so cosy it's almost sleep-inducing - until the food arrives. Start with a fillet of tuna with sesame and honey dressing (€14), followed by the succulent fillet of Irish beef (€28). We love the apple crumble with vanilla ice cream. A tapas menu is also available in the bar until 11pm. P.S. There are over 230 wines to choose from, and Olivier, who managed Thornton's for years, is a passionate guide.

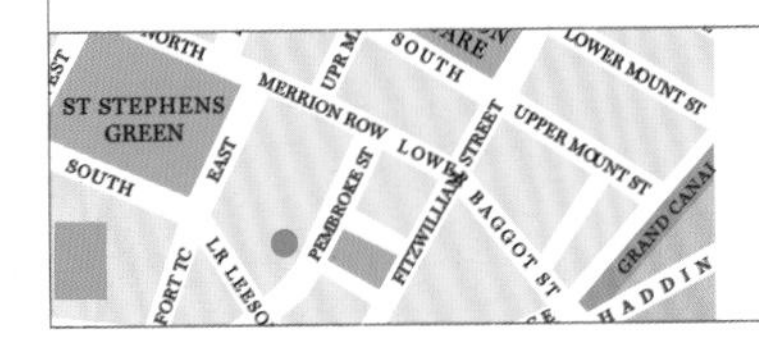


*23 Pembroke Street Upper, Dublin 2.*
*676 1494.*
*www.dax.ie*

# DEEP

*Water Wings*

When we asked owner Brendan O'Connor how he would like his customers to come away, he replied, "Healthier, less wealthier, yet satisfied." He ribbed that food critics are overfed and impossible to excite, and admitted to turfing out well-heeled dames for being obnoxious. Good to see an owner with a love for the common man, especially in this snooty part of Howth. Deep is waterside – but there isn't a floating trolley in sight. The spotless vibe continues indoors, with bright white walls and impressive artwork. Chef Paul McNally does a familiar array of Mediterranean seafood dishes: deep-fried calamari (€7.95) and sea bass (€22.50) are sure things. They also claim to serve "the best buffalo wings on the Northside" (€7.50).

*12 West Pier, Howth,*
*County Dublin.*
*806 3921.*
*www.deep.ie*

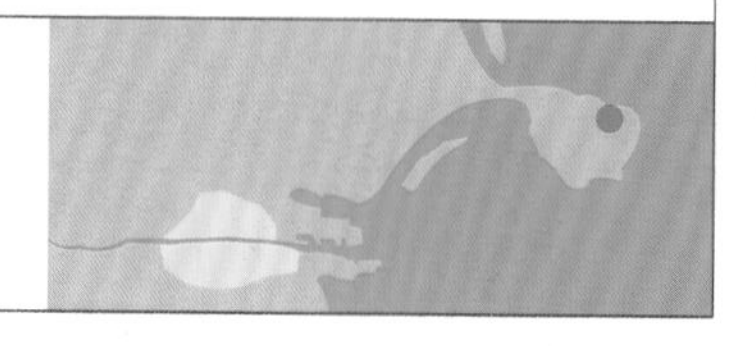

EXPOSED: DUBLIN'S 'BEST' SCHOOLS
The Dubliner
Pig Out!

The Dubliner
GENERATION MUMBO JUMBO
"Sorry, no time for God right now...
...I'm busy with my personal angel."

The insider's guide to Dublin right now
The Dubliner
PUSH
HOW FAR RIGHT CAN THE IRISH TIMES GO?
OVER
BY HARRY BROWNE
REVEALED: IRELAND'S 10 BEST COUNTRY HOTELS
The Dubliner
The Food Issue

YOUR ANNUAL GUIDE TO THE GOOD LIFE
The Dubliner
THE BEST OF DUBLIN 2006

The Dubliner
Ireland's Greatest Artist?
Killing with Kindness
Endgame
Paulo Coelho

RICHARD DAWKINS ON RELIGION
The Dubliner
THE PARTY PEOPLE

The Dubliner
HOW BRIAN O'DRISCOLL MADE
LEINSTER
THE HIPPEST RUGBY TEAM IN EUROPE

The Dubliner
Fancy a drink?
THE 10 BEST BARS IN THE GREATEST DRINKING TOWN ON EARTH

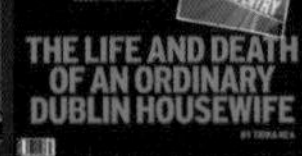
CULTURE OPINION RESTAURANTS HUMOUR ENTERTAINMENT
The Dubliner
"It was the most calculating and callous killing that I have ever encountered."
THE LIFE AND DEATH OF AN ORDINARY DUBLIN HOUSEWIFE

The Dubliner
POLITICS SPECIAL ISSUE
SMART. AMBITIOUS. PASSIONATE.
MAD?

The Dubliner
how to CHANGE YOUR LIFE in 60 seconds

The Dubliner
WEEKEND
NEW POOR
NEW RICH!

The Dubliner
the BEST of DUBLIN
2007

The Dubliner
MAVERICKS!

The Dubliner
Fit for a King!

# DIEP NOODLE

*Ranelagh's Finest*

Thai food suits the Irish palate, with its fresh herbs and just the right level of spiciness – we were never able to handle hot vindaloos like the English. The Diep group still serves the most authentic Thai food in the city, from the flagship Diep Le Shaker, Diep Noodle Bar in Ranelagh and Diep at Home. Where Le Shaker is rich and elegant, Noodle is relaxed and modern, with bright banquettes, red walls and splashed modern art. Book a group table for a Saturday night and try the Taste of Thailand dinner menus – plates of seafood, meat and noodle dishes to share, €36.50 or €38.50 – washed down with a good cocktail. Cheap enough, boisterous and *very* tasty.

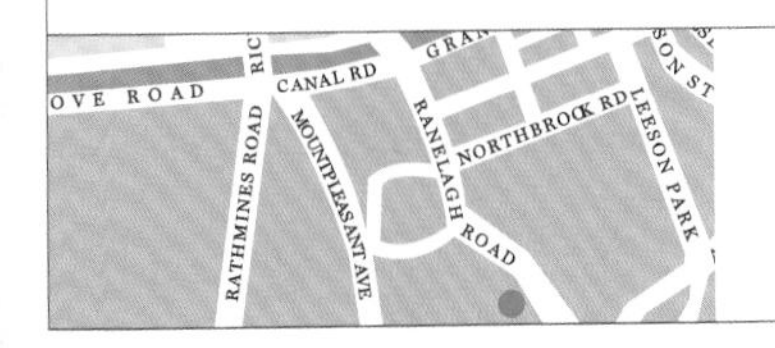


*Ranelagh Village,*
*Dublin 6.*
*497 6550.*
*www.diep.net*

# DOBBINS

*Fat Cat*

This adworld legend earns a place in the *100 Best* for sentimental reasons. Under the late John O'Byrne, one expected a warm, conspiratorial buzz and average food. John has passed away, sadly, and the restaurant is now reborn as a safe choice for middle management. The main difference between New and Old Dobbins is the disappearance of the old glasshouse annexe at the back, where the inner circle gathered before lunch. No sawdust on the floors either: white walls on one side, and brown on the opposite side, white napery, very plain chairs, tiled floor, and *noise*. The food is still more promising than accomplished. Despite all that, you'll probably have a good night.

*15 Stephen's Lane,*
*Mount Street, Dublin 2.*
*661 9536.*
*www.dobbins.ie*

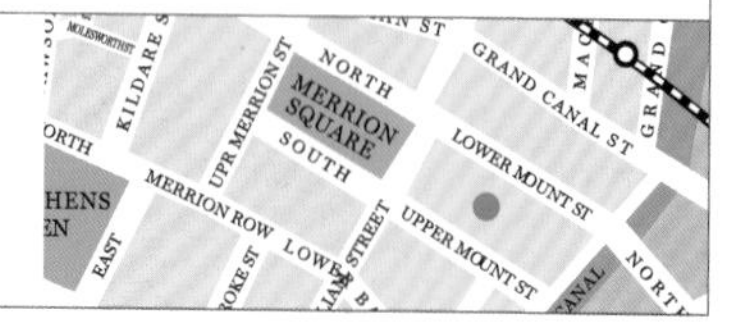

# DUNNE & CRESCENZI

*Ubiquitous Italian*

Eileen Dunne and Stefano Crescenzi moved to Ireland from Rome in 1999 and set up a shop selling fine Italian food and wines. Their business grew to include two restaurants in the city centre, this one in Sandymount, and interests in gems like Nonna Valentina and Bar Italia. They are fans of the slow food movement: it's all about relaxing and enjoying quality, authentic food and wine in a distinctly Italian atmosphere. The Sandymount branch is often packed - don't let them put you upstairs. The menu is short and disjointed, with tasty seasonal dishes and Italian classics like caprese salad (one of *The Dubliner*'s top ten meals for under €10) and hearty bean stew. Slightly chaotic.

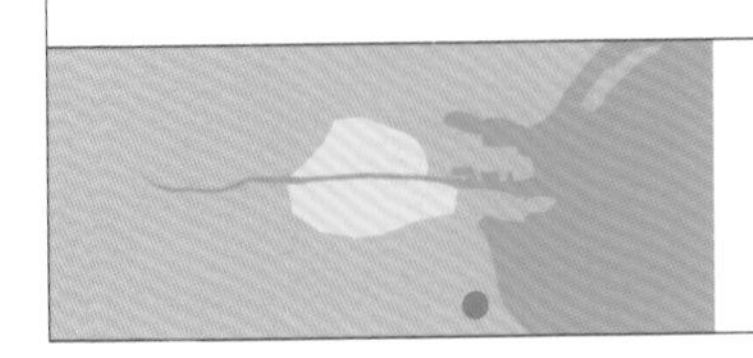

*11 Seafort Avenue, Sandymount, Dublin 4. 667 3252. www.dunneandcrescenzi.com*

# EATERY120

*Quirky Debutant*

This mid-range brasserie has been firing on all cylinders since opening in summer 2007. It's like a suburban Winding Stair: quirky design, simple, interesting food, professional service and a wine list that forgets Columbus discovered the New World. To start, try the sardines on tomato and fennel toast (€9) then the confit of Barbary duck with madeira jus (€21) and follow with strawberry shortcake (€7). The cheeseboard selection is uninspired and one has to wonder if they'll remain as sharp when they're not overstaffed for the sake of caution. It will prosper in Ranelagh, though, filling the gap between chaotic Tribeca and stuffy Mint, and should attract visitors from far afield.

*120 Ranelagh Road,*
*Dublin 6.*
*470 4120.*
*www.eatery120.ie*

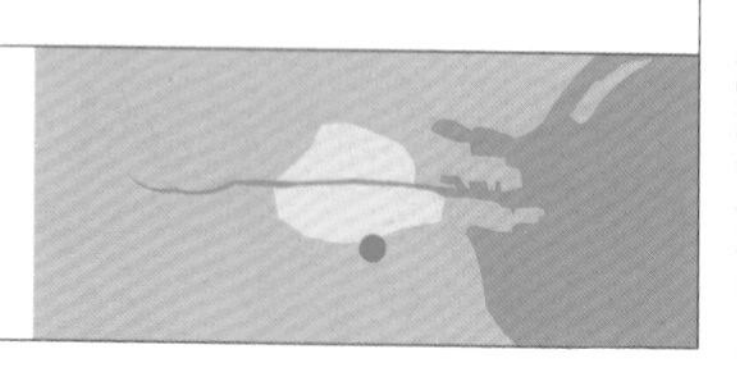

# L'ECRIVAIN

*Peerless*

No restaurant in Ireland owes as much to the singular talents of its key players. On the rare occasions when neither Derry nor Sallyanne Clarke are in evidence, L'Ecrivain seems somewhat hollow, an impressive sarcophagus robbed of king and queen, baubles and trinkets. Fortunately their deputies are well trained – so we get over it and settle down to enjoying the grub. The cooking is stylish but relatively unfussy. Many chefs are playing around with duck legs, slow-cooked pork belly and the like, but none get as close to that modern French experience of *haute couture* comfort food as Derry. Plus: Martina Delaney, a wonderful sommelier, has created a balanced and inventive wine list.

*109a Lower Baggot Street, Dublin 2.*
*661 1919.*
*www.lecrivain.com*

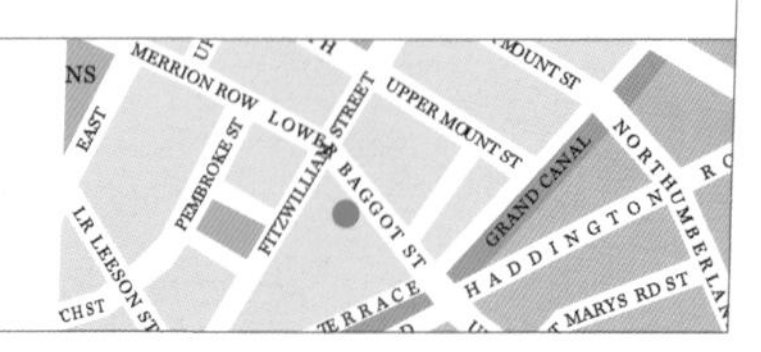

# EDEN

*Best of Temple Bar*

Eleanor Walsh has moved on. She was Eden's guiding spirit. But this two-storey classic remains a cool white haven amid the beer-stained madness of Temple Bar. (Try to get a table downstairs or alfresco on a fine day.) Expect contemporary fare with a hint of traditionalism: the Guinness Stew (€22) is made with organic beef, and we love the herb-crusted rack of lamb with mash and basil jus (€29). Come for brunch on a Saturday. Have the Smokies (€13) – smoked haddock with crème fraîche and cheddar melt – with home fries, and watch the HiCos sniff the avocados in the Temple Bar Market while little Ruan and Fiona stick their fingers in the homemade cakes. You're having a David McWilliams moment.

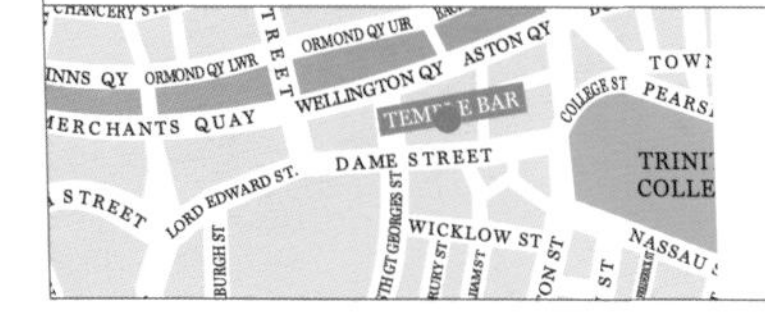


*Meeting House Square,*
*Temple Bar, Dublin 2.*
*670 5372.*
*www.edenrestaurant.ie*

# ELEPHANT & CASTLE

*Chicken Wings!*

**Word has it** that the portions are smaller than before. Maybe we're just getting bigger. Either way, the chicken wings (€12) are still good, good, good. Indeed they're worth the wait, even if it means spending half of your Saturday sitting on that little palm tree watching the chuggers and fire dancers in Temple Bar. (They don't take reservations.) Big, juicy burgers all come in under €13: none of the prices have been hiked too much since Colin Farrell's waitering days. We love the Elephant burger with curried sour cream, bacon, scallions, cheddar and tomato (€12.95). Veggies have a choice of omelettes (from €8.50), salads (from €9.75) and pasta (€13.50) as well as sandwiches and wraps. Loud, busy, lively.

*18 Temple Bar, Dublin 2.*
*679 3121.*
*www.elephantandcastle.ie*

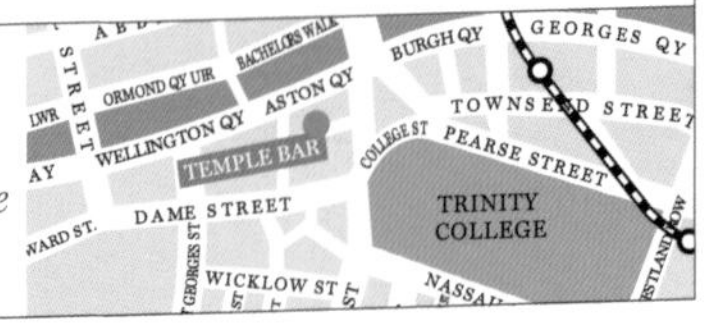

ne things are missing here...

Santa Rita is
one of them.
RESERVA
SAUVIGNON BLANC
CASABLANCA VALLEY · CHILE
Santa Rita

# ELY HQ

*Bourgeois Wine Bar*

We could have picked all three outposts of the Ely empire. Each is a place of mirth and polite excess. This newcomer offers a larger menu than its Ely Place and CHQ sisters, and just as many great wines. There is a hint of the 1960s in the sleek wood, rose-coloured soft furnishings and prints. The menu is weighted towards fish and seafood – starters include Carlingford Oysters (€10), pan-fried lingoustines (€13.50) and scallops carpaccio (€9.95). For mains one might have roast cod fillet with citrus, mint and mussel broth (€23) or pan-roasted halibut (€28.95) – as well as meats sourced from the owners' farm in the Burren. Expect a clued-in, after-work Docklands crowd. Don't be surprised if you score.

*Hanover Quay,*
*Dublin 2.*
*633 9986.*
*www.elywinebar.ie*

# THE EXCHANGE

*Smart Hotel*

The Westin claims to serve "gourmet food at attractive prices." Its restaurant, the Exchange, is on the ground floor. *Leslie Nielsen ate here once.* There's a brasserie vibe for lunch; in the evening it's closer to fine dining. For dinner, try the seared king scallops to start (€16.50), followed by the *feuillete* of poached sea bass, brown crab and asparagus spears with caviar cream (€29). The room preserves the art-deco style of the old bank building, and there are lots of intimate corners for frankly disgusting sex talk. (Ask for table 21.) Afterwards, venture downstairs to the Mint Bar for a cocktail. The Jazz Sunday Brunch, "with unlimited champagne," is naughty but nice.

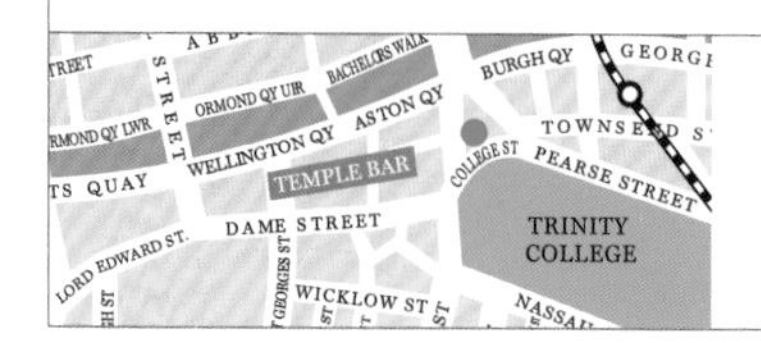


*College Green, Dublin 2.*
*645 1000.*
*www.westin.com*

# FALLON & BYRNE

*Foodie Paradise*

At ground level there is a coffee shop/deli and Dean & Deluca-style food hall, with meat, fish, organic vegetables and many other sundries for the at-home chef. Buy 30-year old Leonardi balsamic vinegar in a bottle that would make Gaultier swoon. The first floor restaurant has a Parisian feel with its long mirrors, stone walls and dark-wood furnishings. Grab a window seat. Expect unpretentious European fare like a sirloin steak with French fries, salad and Béarnaise (€26.50). On Mondays, corkage is just €1 – top deal. We adore the wine cellar in the basement, where you can taste cheese plates and charcuterie, get smashed, meet chic Europeans and pretend it's not raining.

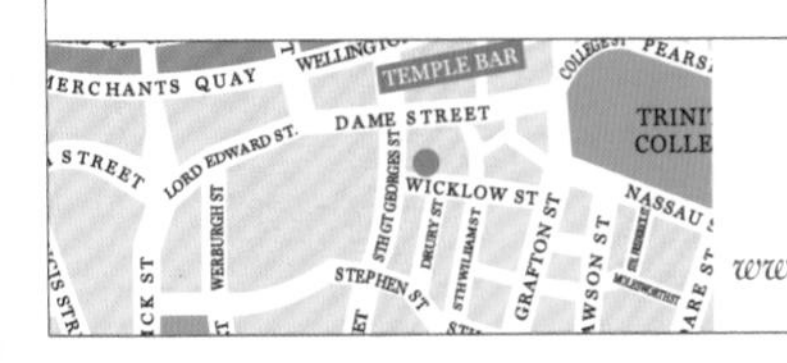


*11-17 Exchequer Street,*
*Dublin 2.*
*472 1010.*
*www.fallonandbyrne.com*

# THE FOUR SEASONS

*Chintz Central*

What a gay dining room! Vast bunches of flowers, alcoves that look over the idyllic garden, coved ceilings, lavish colours and discreet lighting. (Best ladies loos in the county too.) Head chef Terry White is all about seasonal, fresh food. Try the antipasti: a mini feast of insalata caprese, baby shrimp and avocado, calamari with chipotle dip, venison and Serrano ham. All quite expensive, but exquisitely presented and tasty: I had a wonderful broiled *paillard* of salmon. The desserts are fabulous, angelic, made by some pudding god. And speaking of gods, one must pay homage to maitre d' John Healy. Best in the business. P.S. Sunday lunch is celeb-watching time (Is Louis Walsh a celebrity?).

*Simmonscourt Road, Ballsbridge, Dublin 4. 665 4000. www.fourseasons.com/dublin*

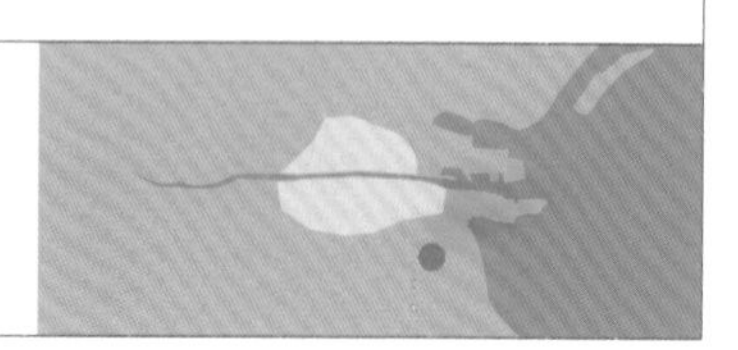

# THE FRENCH PARADOX

*Premier Cru*

An Aladdin's cave for the oenophile. Pierre and Tanya Chapeau – she's posh, he's French – buy directly from small producers, and they can tell you the history of every bottle. Upstairs in the Tasting Room they also serve what is probably best described as upmarket snack food – salads, omelettes, charcuterie, patés and cheeses. Lovely waitresses. Bring a group and get a selection of *assiettes* for the table – they start at €11.90 for a sharing plate. Or go for a couple of tapas-style plates of olives, sausages, ham, fish, meat, washed down with a bloody good red. They're surprisingly filling: a French paradox indeed. And if you like the taste of something, don't forget that it's all available to take home.

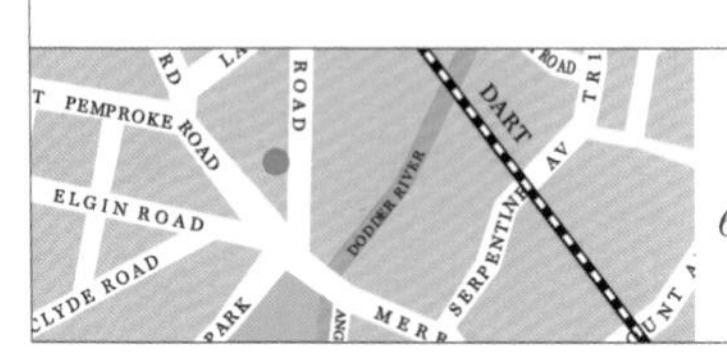


*53 Shelbourne Road, Ballsbridge, Dublin 4. 660 4068. www.thefrenchparadox.com*

# GEORGES

*Pre-Renards*

The best things about this basement wine bar and bistro in the shadow of Renards nightclub are a.) a smoker-friendly patio with rich red walls, and b.) a splendid pianist. We have never been that impressed by the food, and, while it is improving, there is still a sense that the chef is over-reaching. If the paté de foie gras in the hamburger made any difference to its taste, one would feel obliged to reward imagination. A fillet of beef with sautéed potatoes took an hour to arrive. Our waitress was a young Italian student whose smile made it difficult to carp with any conviction. Good spot for a glass of something en route to the fleshpots. (Are you aware that Dunne & Crescenzi is across the road?)

*12 South Frederick Street, Dublin 2.*
*617 0900.*
*www.trinitylodge.com*

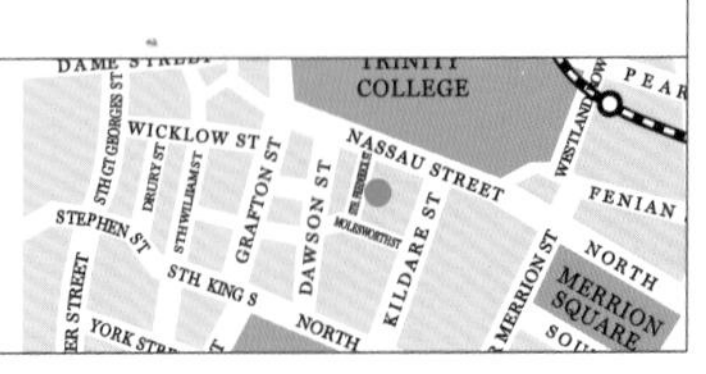

# GOTHAM

*Veteran Pizza Joint*

It's surprisingly hard to find a decent mid-range bite in the city centre: we can't count the number of times we've stood scratching our heads on Grafton Street, surrounded by sandwich bars and cafés that are packed every lunchtime for no good reason. Thank goodness for Gotham. Sit inside and pinpoint when it all went wrong on the *Rolling Stone* covers that line the walls. Or sit outside amid the shopping madness: see it all going wrong live. Very baby-friendly – too much so if you have a hangover – and lovely staff. The pizzas are just fine. We like the Midtown: spicy and thin with mushrooms, red onion, baby corn, sweet peppers, garlic and mozzarella (€11.25).

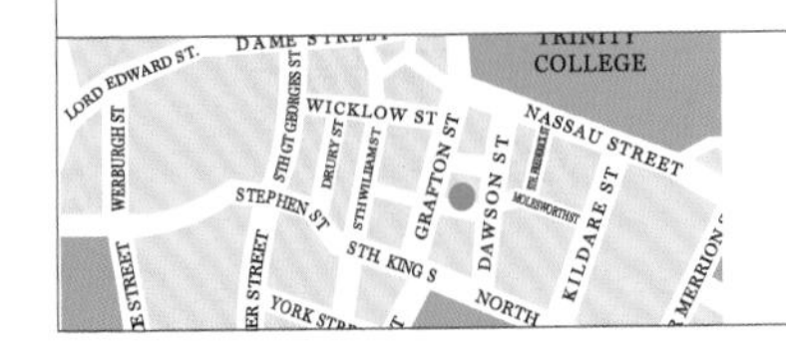


*8 South Anne Street,*
*Dublin 2.*
*679 5266*

# GRUEL

*Eccentric & Lovable*

Ah, Gruel! Behind the counter it's Billy Scurry, chef and DJ in no particular order. We ask for the fish soup, salad and a slice of goat's cheese pizza. It's lunchtime and the ground floor is packed tighter than a tin of sardines in extra virgin olive oil, so we head downstairs. In the basement, we pull up to a rickety table. The food arrives. The fish soup is hearty, hot, with a subtle tingle. The pizza? Well, we like our pizza like a *Carry On* film, and although this one has a heady amount of cheese, it's not saucy enough. The salad elicits gasps and moaning, in a good way. Gruel has been a fixture on the daytime scene since Temple Bar was cool. It remains *a very funky place.* P.S. Best lunchtime rolls in town.

*68a Dame Street,*
*Dublin 2.*
*670 7119*

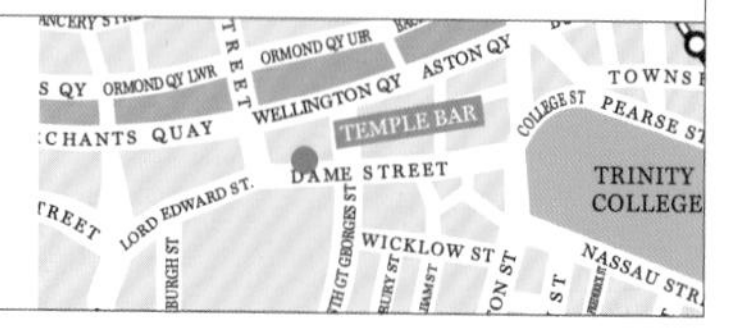

# L'GUEULETON

*Last Year's Love*

For a long time I thought, 'why bother?' The name is ridiculous, it was up-its-bum cool, and they didn't take bookings. But once I finally made it into l'Gueuleton - for lunch, quite a bit easier to get a table - all was forgiven. It's classy and informal, with high ceilings and low lights, the tables close enough for neighbourly smiles but not uncomfortably packed. The menu is classic, provincial French – the food is not quite as cheap as it was in Troy Maguire's heyday, and not as exciting, either. There is a short but sufficient, all-French wine list and they do great desserts (each €7). The service is almost laughably erratic; sometimes charming, sometimes aloof.

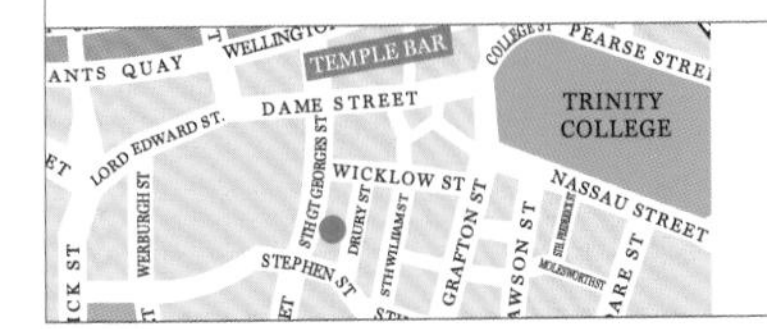


*1 Fade Street, Dublin 2.*
*675 3708*

# HALO

*Once-hip Hotel*

Hugh O'Regan's first hotel project is still one of the city's more stylish addresses. It feels neither as youthful as it once did nor quite as chic. However, it remains a popular spot for cocktails among "30-45 years old with good disposable income." (Gavin Lambe-Murphy is a regular. Seriously.) The restaurant never seemed to live up to the rest of the hotel's standards. But a recent facelift and the arrival of Richie Wilson, previously of Thornton's, are encouraging signs. Halo is large, warm, lively when it's full (and all too lonesome when it's not). The signature dish is a roast five spice magret duck breast with tortellini of confit duck leg, sherry vinegar and orange sauce (€26.95).

*Lower Ormond Quay, Dublin 1.*
*887 2400. www. morrisonhotel.ie*

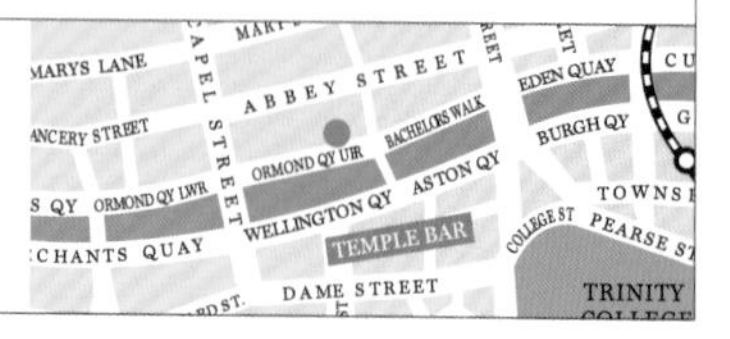

# HARVEY NICHOLS

*Retail Therapy*

Meet Ross O'Carroll-Kelly's mum on a blowout shopping trip to Dundrum Town Centre. Then have lunch in Harvey Nics. Very New York: slick, open-plan and boldly contemporary, there are slouchy leather couches and a bold pink cocktail bar. Have a "First Floor Smash" – strawberries, cointreau, lemon and sugar topped with champagne. Try Thomas Haughton's marinated loin of spring lamb (€28), or pot roast belly of pork with honey and coriander, roast turnip and parsnip purée (€26). Fine set lunch or early dinner for €25, impressive wine list, great service and guest DJs at the weekend – a perfect way to burn off the calories. Tables 180 and 181 have the best views.

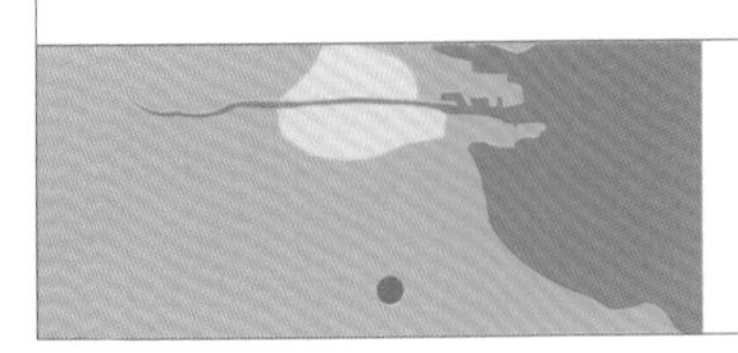

*Dundrum Town Centre,*
*Sandyford Road,*
*Dublin 16. 291 0488.*
*www.harveynichols.com*

# HEMMINGWAYS

*Fish Shop*

Why the name? Lord knows, except that old Ernie was quite a fisherman. And why the double 'm'? Dyslexia maybe; or because there's a Hemingways (no relation) on the Southside. Anyway, who cares? There should be a preservation order on this place. It's not a restaurant, it's a fish shop with ranks of stools. Book well in advance. The grub is marine-flavoured – fish or squid tapas, paella, bouillabaisse, chowder etc. Or select a chunk of fresh fish from the slab and have it cooked and served with your choice of sauce. Things have taken a slight dip since the peripatetic Kiwi ex-trawlerman/chef slung his hook, but it's still good and prices are fair.

*2b Vernon Avenue,*
*Clontarf,*
*Dublin 3.*
*833 3338*

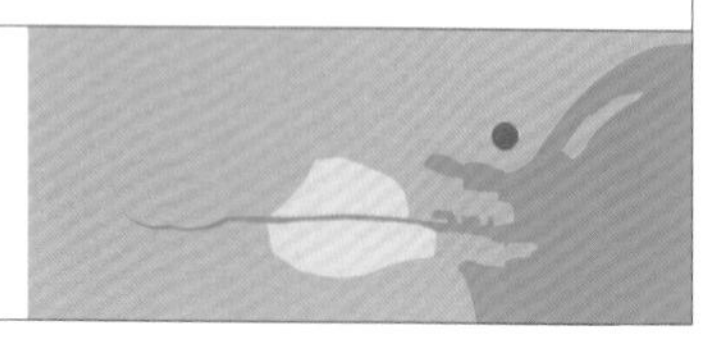

# INDIE SPICE

*Flash Indian*

Owner Tariq Salahuddin spent €30,000 to get two cast members of *Coronation Street* to attend the launch of his grandiose Indian. Everything in here is big; the tables, the chairs, the kitchen and of course, the menu. One of three branches – the others are in Naas and Belfast – it offers a typical array of Indian dishes – and some not so typical – in big portions. Try the duck *malai* kebab (€17.95): succulent and memorable to the very last forkful. Mohammed Adnan's signature dish is jumbo prawns in coconut milk and spices (€19.95). You can also get carry-out with the Indie at Home service. Finally, there is a decent (if somewhat safe) Sunday lunch menu at €18.50 for three courses.

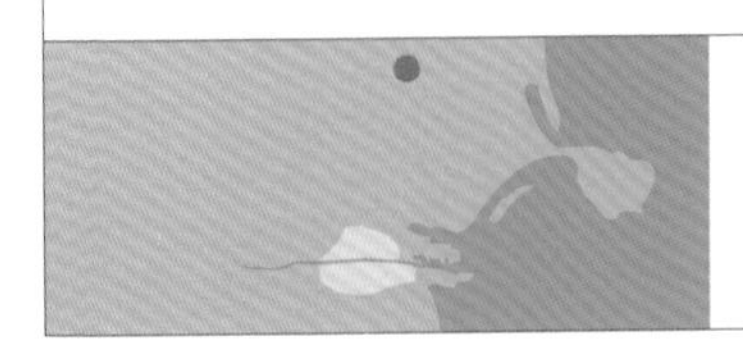

*Burgundy House, New Street, Swords, County Dublin. 807 7999. www.indiespicecafe.com*

# ITSA4

*An Old Friend*

Domini and Peaches Kemp are attractive, funny, smart girls. In addition to their popular bagel empire, the Kemp sisters are restaurateurs, food critics, champion golfers and international showjumpers. (Only a slight exaggeration.) This tiny place in Sandymount is their mothership. It's where flavours are tossed about with elegant determination, and where groups of women start singing after dinner. It's where the staff of *The Dubliner* go to wind down. It's where PRs, Republicans, journalists and bus conductors come to eat casually, among friends. Go for dinner on a Tuesday, or for Sunday brunch after a walk along the South Wall. Come in a group, or aim to make friends. It's a blast.

*6a Sandymount Green,*
*Dublin 4.*
*219 4676.*
*www.itsabagel.com*

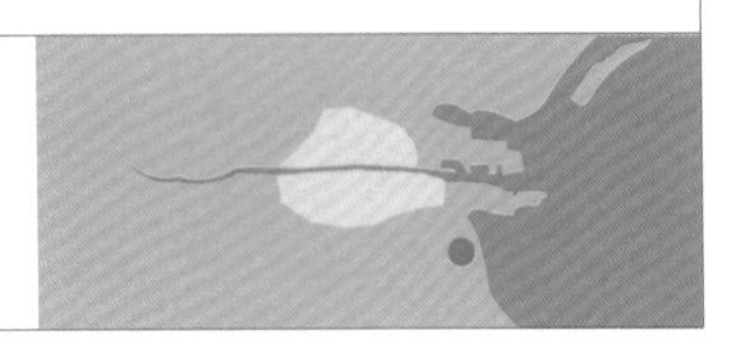

# IVORY

*Trendy Bar*

Dalkey gets a lot of criticism. I used to be one of the begrudgers. I'm a sensitive Northsider. But I'm going out with a Southsider. This led me to cross the river and head down to Ivory on a Friday night with a few of my Dalkey acquaintances. I know, how cosmopolitan. Ivory is a bar/restaurant serving reasonable food in computer-designed surroundings. I could almost visualise the designer's 3D mock-up: "This is where we'll have the sculpted wall lit by the mauve mood lighting, and yes those cushions are the same colour as the condiments sets!" The food is satisfactory. Colin Farrell was sitting in the corner nursing an OJ. You know what? Dalkey is full of bleedin' Northsiders.

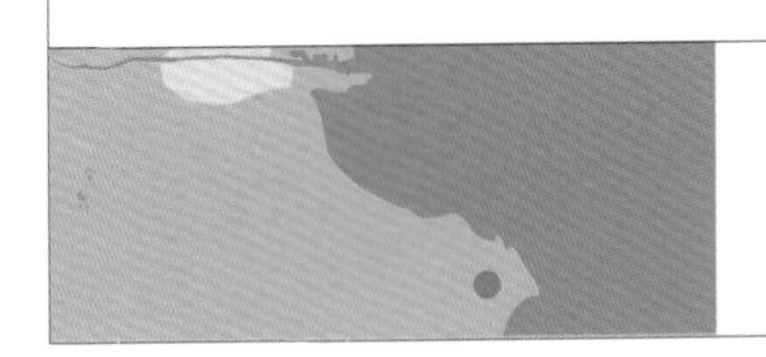

*61 Castle Street, Dalkey,*
*County Dublin.*
*235 2153*

# JADE

*Dinner for a Song*

Don't be afraid when searching for this little charmer. Hidden off the top of Capel Street, Jade is at its best late at night, catering for large karaoke-focused rabbles. Unlike the posh Southside karaoke bars, these guys don't charge for the use of the rooms. You are left alone in (spartan) surroundings with a buzzer to call for help if you or the video machine goes on the blink. Food is good, plentiful and refreshingly odd: are they the only restaurant in the city to serve fried dumplings? Order the *yu-xiang* aubergines, the spicy fish stew and the twice-fried pork. Cheap! And don't feel embarrassed when you're leaving – you weren't half as rowdy as we were.

*27 Little Mary Street, Dublin 1. 887 4468*

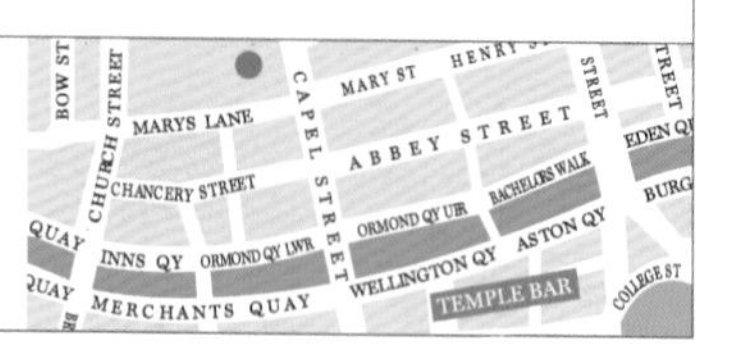

# JAIPUR

*Swanky Indian*

Asheesh Dewan is the debonair proprietor of a Michelin-starred stunner on Berkeley Square, London, called Benares. Here in Dublin he owns five outposts of an empire, Jaipur, that is slowly educating the Irish palate – it's an adventure that brings exotic new life to suburbs such as Dalkey, Greystones and Ongar. The future of the flagship on South Great Georges Street is uncertain. This Malahide branch is small – 42 seats – but the Indian cooking could not be more expansive. Ask chef Amubhav to throw away the rulebook. Warm service. P.S. Good news for locals. Jaipur is soon to be joined in Malahide by Kinara, an offshoot of the Anglo-Pakistani restaurant in Clontarf.

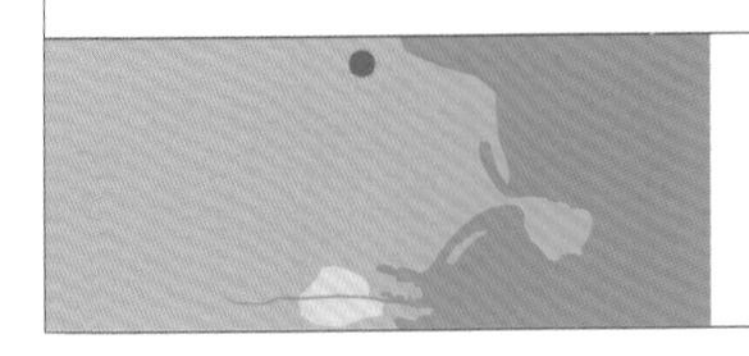

*5, St James Terrace, Malahide, County Dublin. 845 5455. www.jaipur.ie*

# JO'BURGER

*Rathmines Rocks*

What's to love? Organic burgers, the DJ, a slick interior and lots of old school board games. Doesn't sound like Dublin, right? Here, the tunes are cooler than a double frosted cherry popsicle on the first day of your summer holidays and the menus are made from *Beano* annuals; check out the *aaarghs, harumphs* and *eeks* while you decide which of the burger-shared options to go for. We love the *moroko* (bacon and brie) and the *chiawelo* (fresh mango salsa and rocket.) All sound odd, many are delicious. Perfect spot for a date, or just hanging with your mates. Plus: they're open late on a Saturday night if the anxiety of the pub doesn't appeal and you still want to get your groove on.

*137 Rathmines Road,*
*Rathmines, Dublin 6.*
*491 3731.*
*www.joburger.ie*

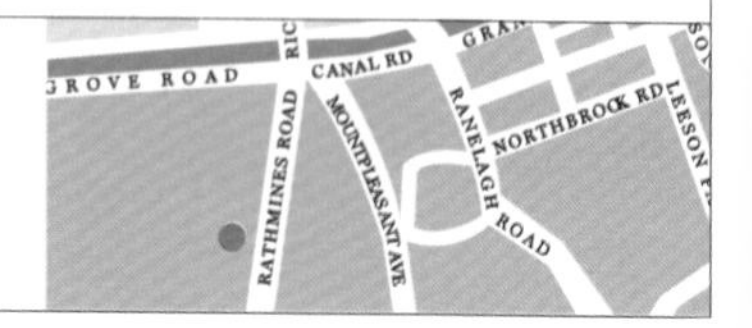

pick and mix
MB GAMES
GUESS WHO?
Identify the mystery face!
Make & Play
MINIATURE DOLL CRAFT
MB GAMES
GUESS WHO?
The mystery face game
MB GAMES
OPERATION
ELECTRONIC
CHINESE CHEQUERS
BATTLE PICTURE
ACTION ANNUAL
THE BEEZER BOOK
CASTLE LAGER
REKORDERLIG
VEDETT
BATTLE PICTURE WEEKLY ANNUAL 1982
WHOOPEE! ANNUAL 1983
WARLORD FOR BOYS
THE BEEZER BOOK

# JOHNNIE FOX'S

*Kelly's Book Fare*

There is something incorrigibly naff about the very idea of Johnnie Fox's. Billed as a culinary and musical theme park, it is popular among the sort of Americans who think green beer is acceptable. Yet there is no doubting the sincerity of the hospitality up here in Glencullen. Indeed the quality of the reception is not the only notable attraction. Massive plates of fresh seafood, steaks and sundry roasts are all good hearty fare, and as long as you're not driving, there are few more charming places for a pint and a chat with perfect strangers. (If all this wears you out, head over to the Blue Light for a different view of Dublin and a vibe that some find all too real.)

*Glencullen, County Dublin.*
*295 5647.*
*www.jfp.ie*

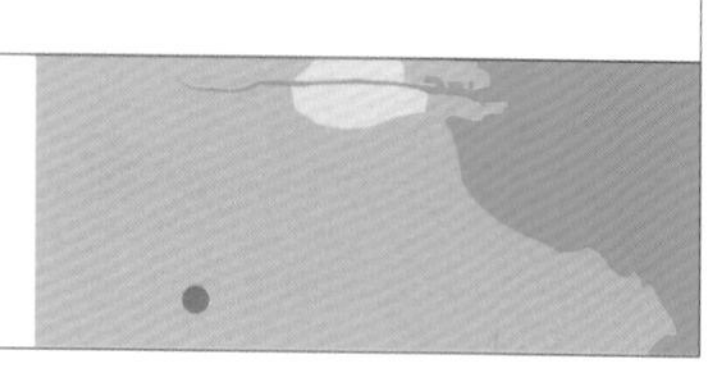

# KC PEACHES

*Upmarket Deli*

Secure the coveted couch in KC Peaches and pretend you're living in that Manhattan loft you've always dreamed about. This lunch spot feels cosy: lots of wood and floor-to-ceiling radiators. The laptop-clutching fund accountants are a permanent fixture; with the Docklands facelift well under way and prices rising, they may be renting office space here. Lots of staff, but they're slightly disorganised. Persevere – it's worth it. On a cold day have the tomato and mature cheddar soup, a meal in itself. The pasta salad in a spicy satay sauce is a must. Sandwiches and melts are vastly superior to most sandwich shops. Good value. Mediocre coffee, so buy a pecan brownie for later instead.

*Trinity Enterprise Centre,*
*Pearse Street, Dublin 2.*
*677 0333.*
*www.kcpeaches.com*

# LANGKAWI

*Functional Malaysian*

Good ethnic restaurants in Dublin are still thin on the ground. Malaysian ones more so. Alex Hosey opened Langkawi in 1984, when it must have seemed a curiosity indeed. Langkawi is not exceptional but at least it's honest, by which we mean the food is 'of the region,' uncomplicated, unmucked about with and in no way dumbed down. The ambience is clubby; management and staff have a way of making people feel welcome so the restaurant has built up a loyal following. Latterly prices seem to have escalated, making Langkawi not quite the value-for-money trip it once was. The provision of coffee as the third course in a three-course lunch seems a bit of a nose-thumb too.

*46 Upper Baggot St,*
*Dublin 4.*
*668 2760*

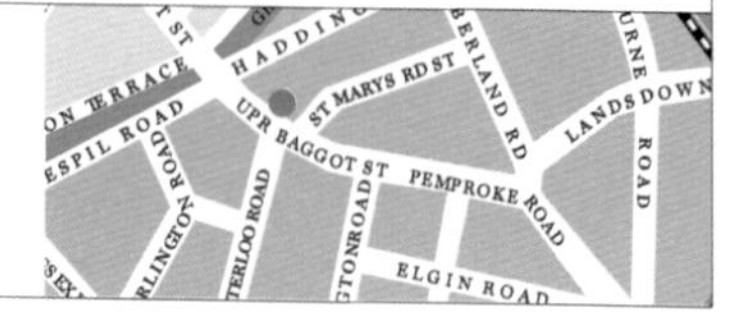

# LÉON

*Handsome Café*

Tom Doorley gave this upmarket café a rave review in the *Irish Times*: "I'll be going back to Léon, probably regularly. That's if I can get in, because I have a feeling that it's going to be very busy." At first glance the great man's comments seem a bit generous. Doorley has long championed Penny Plunkett, who worked for Patrick Guilbaud before founding La Maison des Gourmets. Today she is a consultant for Léon. Even Penny admits that the three outlets – all within 100 yards of each other – are "very similar" to a French café chain, Paul. To be fair, the food is all, as Tom says, well-above average, and the room itself has charm. Not, then, the best new restaurant of the year, but certainly worthy of some small praise.

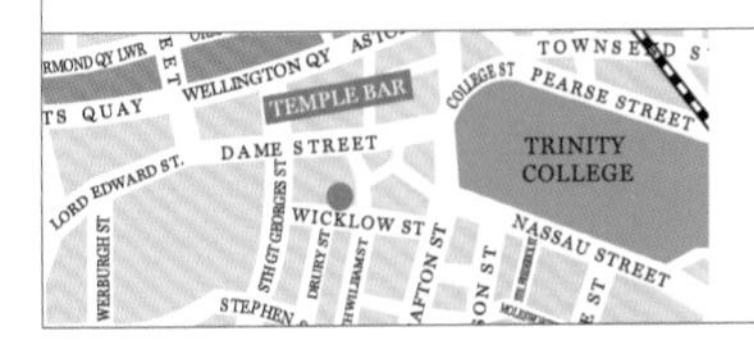


*33 Exchequer Street,*
*Dublin 2.*
*670 7238.*
*www.cafeleon.ie*

# THE LOBSTER POT

*Old School Fish*

When people ask us to suggest somewhere charming but old-fashioned, we recommend places like Hunter's Hotel and the Lord Edward. The Lobster Pot always gets a mention too. This small, pokey first floor restaurant is owned and managed by an old-school gent called Tommy Crean. His team of veteran waiters may seem cold or slightly formal initially, but as the evening wears on you will realise that you are actually in the hands of old pros. This is gracious dining, and the only thing to eat is fish. Admire the theatrical relish with which the catch of the day is presented. Sit back, smile and check you brought your wallet. Everything is right in the world.

*9 Ballsbridge Terrace,*
*Dublin 4. 668 0025.*
*www.thelobsterpot.ie*

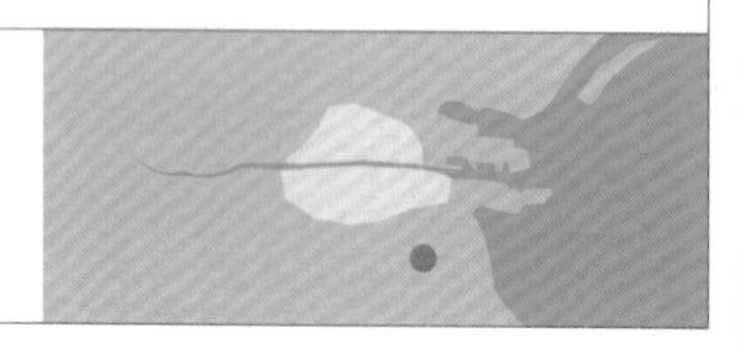

# LOCKS

*Canalbank Treat*

The best restaurant reborn in 2007. Troy Maguire has brought from L'Gueuleton a menu of simple French bistro food, though ingredients here are "more extravagant." Wild mushrooms, truffles, turbot and prawns – call it bistro-luxe. Downstairs is lighter but also more austere than it once was, with white linen, off-white walls, hip lamps, tea candles and a hardwood floor. To start, try the prawns with pigeon biscuit, cep, celeriac and roquette (€16.90). Portions are comically huge: the hors d'oeuvres plate could serve as a grand lunch, while a black pudding and apple tart tatin (€13) was surely conceived for Homer Simpson. The portions will hardly remain this big. Let's hope Maguire stays.

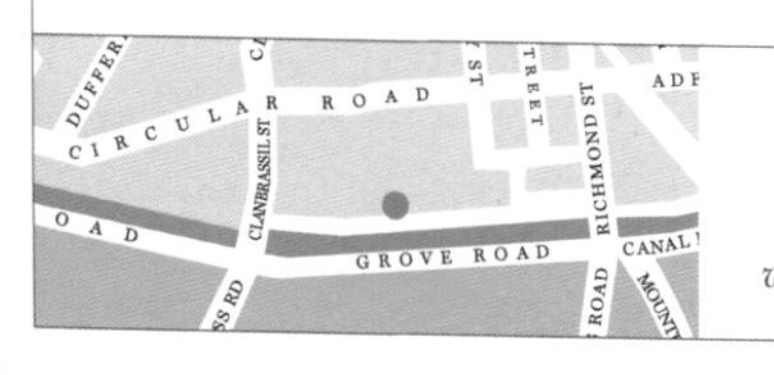


*1 Windsor Terrace,*
*Portobello, Dublin 8.*
*454 3391.*
*www.locksrestaurant.ie*

# THE LORD EDWARD

*A Survivor*

Nothing new to report here. Our oldest seafood restaurant still seems almost primeval, and that is part of its charm. To dine here, you have to schlep up two flight of stairs in a building that dates from the 18th Century, before entering a dining room that feels unchanged since the time of John Charles McQuaid. Many of the staff trained in the old Russell Hotel, and their age shows in dishes such as the Sole Lord Edward, in which the fish is steamed, garnished with prawns, white wine and lobster sauce, and stuffed with smoked salmon. The average price of dinner for two, including a bottle of the house white, is about €105. Venture downstairs for a pint with the auld lads afterwards.

*23 Christchurch Place,*
*Dublin 8.*
*454 2420.*
*www.lordedward.ie*

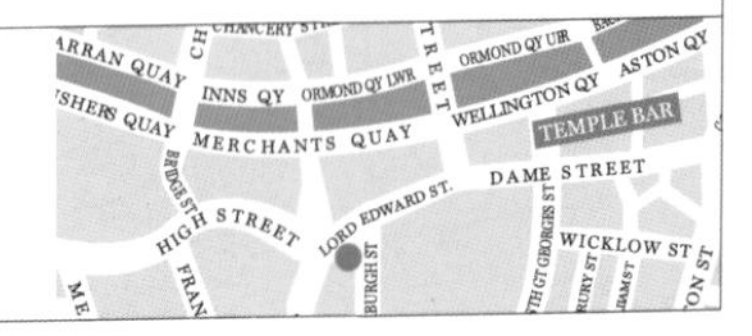

# MAO

*Budget Asian*

It's not quite an empire, but it's certainly heading that way. From its flagship on Chatham Row, Mao has conquered Dublin, Glasgow and Cape Town. This Dundrum branch is allegedly "the jewel in the crown." It's by the pond outside Dundrum Town Centre – sit outside on a nice evening. Inside is bright and funky, with a touch of the fast-food vibe in the functional furniture, and in the food. Expect a mix of Indonesian, Thai and Chinese cuisine. Fresh and zippy soups, tiger prawns, crayfish salad, chilli squid and satay chicken are all under €8. For mains, try the Malaysian chicken (€18.95) or the chilli mango duck with *hokkien* noodles (€17.95). One for after the cinema.

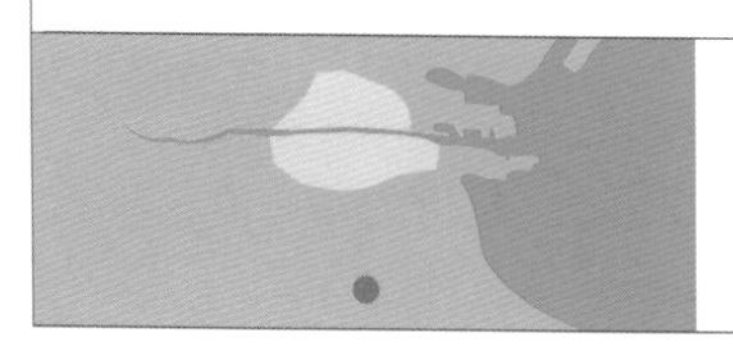

*Civic Square,*
*Dundrum Town Centre,*
*Dublin 16. 296 2802.*
*www.cafemao.com*

# THE MERMAID

*Mid-Atlantic*

Ben Gormley and Mark Harrell, a chef and an artist, have had the Mermaid for 11 years, making it an enduring symbol of the mid-90s Dublin documented in, say, *About Adam*. Gormley and co-chef Ian Connolly's food is called "mid-Atlantic" – yes, that is drivel. There are always lots of fish and seafood options – the crab cakes (€10.95) are good enough to have earned a permanent spot on the menu. Last time, we ate roast John Dory with sauté potatoes. Simple and very tasty. It's pricey enough, but if you have a few hours to wallow and people-watch, there are few finer spots in the area. What else? Fine service, popular for Sunday brunch, and a good-value lunch menu. *Uncomfortable chairs!*

*69-70 Dame Street,*
*Dublin 2.*
*670 8236.*
*www.mermaid.ie*

# THE MERRION

*Uber-Luxe*

The daunting presence of Patrick Guilbaud overshadows other dining options in the Merrion: the ornate drawing room (posh lunches), the Cellar bar (gourmet pub grub), the Cellar restaurant (full dinner menu) and the terrace overlooking the garden. If you have the weather, head to the latter and nibble canapés, finger sandwiches, fresh pastries and scones for €32 – add champagne to the mix for €49.50. Godlike staff. Sunday brunch in the Cellar is a treat. Unusually considering the surroundings, there's a corner of goodies for the kids, so you can sip/gulp bubbly without worrying about the little ones, which is what Sundays are all about.

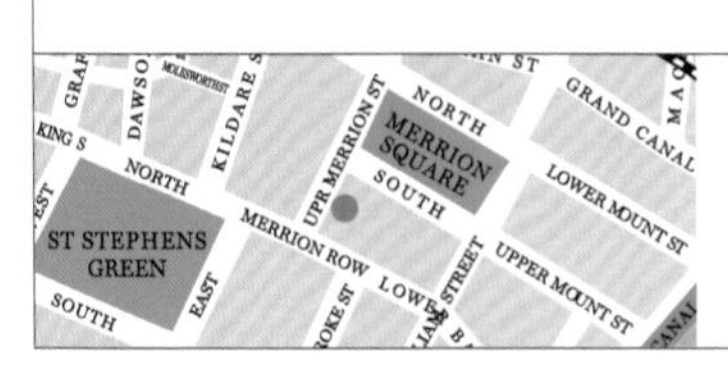


*21 Upper Merrion Street, Dublin 2.*
*603 0600.*
*www.merrionhotel.com*

# MINT

*Wildly Talented*

Dylan McGrath rang up to boast. I am, he said, the most exciting thing happening in an Irish kitchen right now. McGrath had just taken the reins at Mint, a small, pokey restaurant in Ranelagh. McGrath, who is fascinated by Conrad Gallagher, has an intense, slightly awkward manner. He is not a people person in the tradition of, say, Derry Clarke. However, he is every bit as talented, and Mint has since become the most fashionable address in culinary Dublin. I took clients for dinner last night. We spent their annual advertising budget on a truly sublime feast for three people. Most of the customers looked old, rich and determined to spend it all. I don't blame them.

*47 Ranelagh Village,*
*Dublin 6.*
*497 8655.*
*www.mintrestaurant.ie*

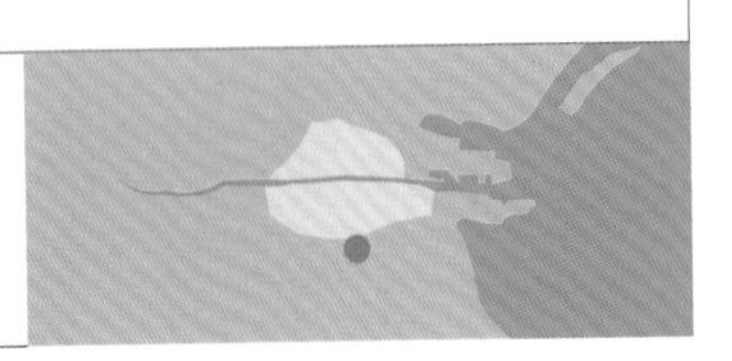

# MONTY'S OF KATHMANDU

*Tibetan Refuge*

Owner Shiva Gautam trained his cousin in Kathmandu before hiring him as head chef of this Nepalese restaurant which he opened in 1997. Shiva is there at the door this afternoon. "Are you sure you're open?" "Yes, although this is mainly an evening sort of place." Correct. Still, I had a respectable two-course lunch for €20, and will return, even if I am the only person there. I had poleko squid, something of a rarity, one assumes, in a landlocked, mountainous kingdom. It is delicious. I followed this with a lamb curry with cauliflower. Go for dinner with a gang of friends – come away pleased, not ripped off, and gasp at the fact that it's possible to eat this well in Temple Bar.

*28 Eustace Street,*
*Temple Bar, Dublin 2.*
*670 4911.*
*www.montys.ie*

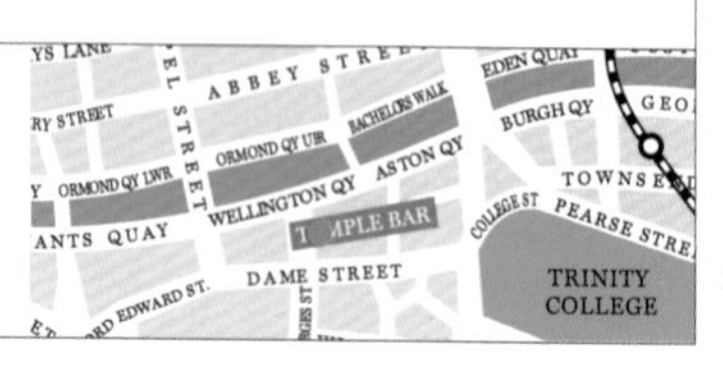

# NONNA VALENTINA

*Portobello Italian*

The Irish absorbed lasagne and spaghetti Bolognese (though in Bologna they prefer tagliatelle) into our diets via self-styled 'Irish Italian Restaurants' located on or near Dame Street. Eileen Dunne and Stefano Crescenzi upped the ante by proving that 'Italian' could mean something other than 'red sauce.' Nonna Valentina is the couple's most upmarket rendezvous, which is to say 'not very.' One might be dining in any Italian town. Try the carpaccio of tuna (€12) and the fettucce (a thicker style of fettucine) with spicy Irish venison (€13). Drink the house wines. Attack the tiramisu, best in town. Relish the decent espresso. Dammit, this *is* Italy. (Complete with garish lighting.)

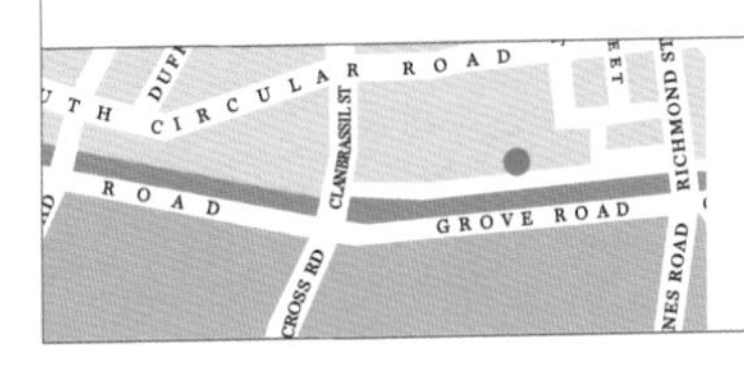


*1 Portobello Road, Portobello, Dublin 8. 454 9866. www. dunneandcrescenzi.com*

# NOSH

*Little Charmer*

Sisters Sacha and Samantha Farrell are all about "big flavoured, unpretentious food with an atmosphere to match." Cheers to that, especially in snooty old Dalkey. Come here for curious fare like prawn pil-pils in sizzling garlic, chili oil and white wine (€9.95), fish and chips (€13.50) and panfried lambs liver and kidneys with champ (€22.50). Yum. They do a popular brunch too – it's buzzy in a good way, unless you're particularly hungover. (Best table sober or drunk is number 6.) Get the DART out on a Sunday, give the cheese steak sandwich (€14.95) a whirl with a nice glass of Red Belly Black Shiraz. Then have a stroll around Dublin's prettiest village and a pint in the Queen's.

*111 Coliemore Road,*
*Dalkey, County Dublin.*
*284 0666.*
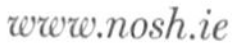
*www.nosh.ie*

# NUDE

*Happy Hippie*

Simple idea: fast food with soul. And it works. Organic wraps and nutritious 'quickies' appeal to yoga moms, rushing suits and skaters with the munchies. Canteen vibe. Long benches make it easy to chat up yer one with the wheatgrass shot (but not so easy to escape yer man with the spinach in his teeth). Order the Berry Burst smoothie and the Thai green curry wrap (€5.75). All about the vitamins. Uniquely for a fast-food joint, you won't find anything processed. Bono's big bro Norman Hewson – "a frustrated helicopter pilot" – is the owner. Norm keeps the U2 boys in food when they're recording. Not very rock and roll, but still. (By the way, there's a slightly emaciated Nude in the airport. What's *that* about?)

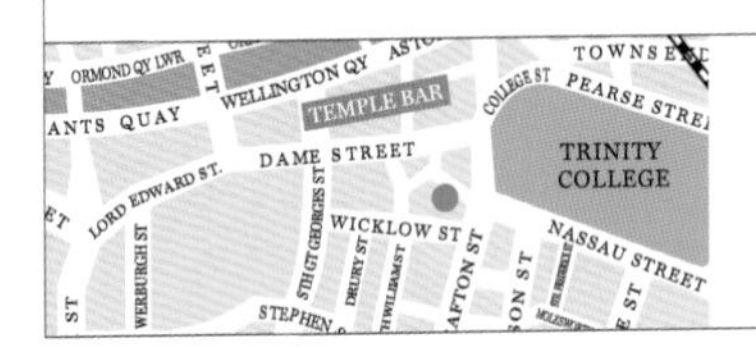


*21 Suffolk Street,*
*Dublin 2.*
*677 4310.*
*www.nude.ie*

# O'CONNELLS

*Darina Allen's Brother*

A hotel restaurant – and *not* our favourite hotel. Tom O'Connell set up shop in the basement of a budget Bewley's eight years ago. His restaurant is very family- and group-friendly, but the massive space is now divided, so you can *usually* find a quiet corner. O'Connell's culinary hero is Myrtle Allen, his sister Darina's mother-in-law, and he shares her passion for tasty, nutritious Irish food – the kind you wish you had time to prepare yourself at home, as O'Connell says. Try the organic chicken pot pie. Sunday lunch offers real value: you can eat as much as you like for just €22.75 and kids pay €1 per year of age, which leads to "healthy dishonesty" on the Sabbath.

*Bewley's Hotel,*
*Ballsbridge, Dublin 4.*
*647 3304. www.oconnells*
*ballsbridge.com*

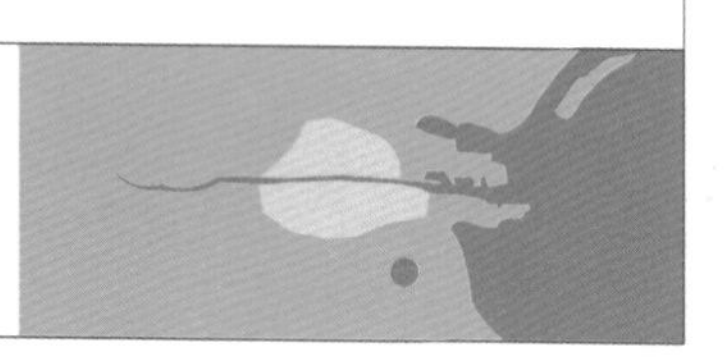

# ODESSA

*Newpark Types*

Still the King of the weekend brunch. Come with the *Guardian* review and a craving for eggs Benedict and a hair-of-the-dog mimosa. Prices are still reasonable, with all brunch options under a tenner, and the buzzing upstairs and comfy downstairs both appeal to hipsters. You still can't book for peak brunch time, but the wait doesn't seem to be as bad these days. Dinner is a different experience: lights down, pan-pipe music up and it all feels vaguely romantic. There's often something quirky – shark, kangaroo – along with fish specials, good steaks and veggie options. Cocktails a plus here, and the wine list is extensive with many decent options under the €30 mark.

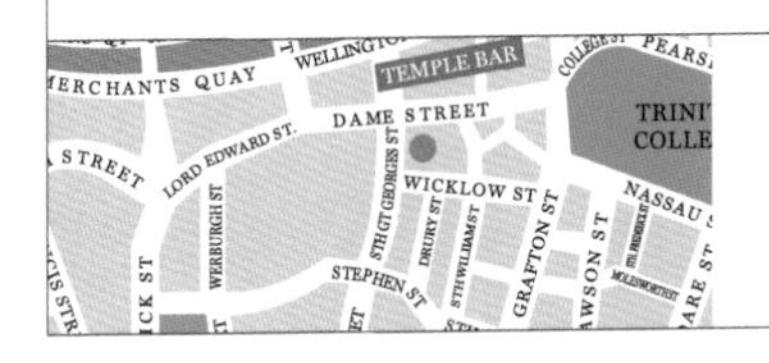


*14 Dame Court,*
*Dublin 2.*
*670 7634.*
*www.odessa.ie*

# PATRICK GUILBAUD

*Michelin Mastery*

Misers diss Guilbaud's - it's expensive - and yes, most of us wait for a rich uncle to pop his clogs before we eat here. Nevertheless, there are bargains to be found, like the €90 whole Challans duck for two - if you bought a Challans duck in Challans, it would probably cost you €40. And the two-course lunch for €35 is, in its way, remarkable value. The service is well up to the two-Michelin-star mark, and this in itself costs big bucks. If we diss them, it's only because we have no rich relatives or because we don't get orgasmic about a waiter's ability to intercept a napkin in freefall. All the same, we are lucky to have Monsieur Giblets. (P.S That's head chef Guillaume Lebrun in the picture. Cheerful lad.)

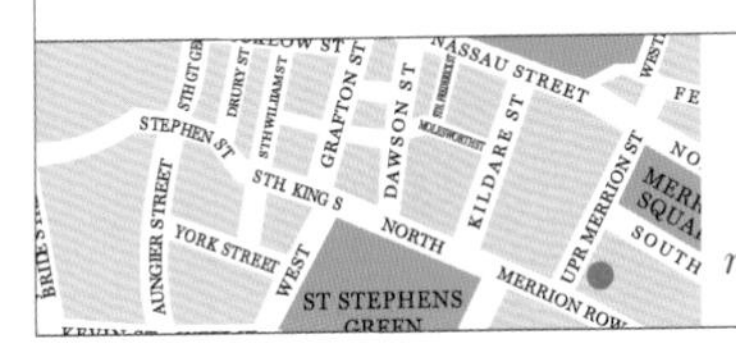


*The Merrion Hotel, 21 Merrion Street Upper, Dublin 2. 676 4192. www.restaurantpatrickguilbaud.ie*

# LA PENICHE

*Supper on a Boat?*

Could it be the shopping trolleys? Somehow canals don't say 'romance' here the way they do in Paris or Venice. That notion is challenged by this bistro-on-a-barge – don't worry, it's quite roomy below decks. Many ingredients are organic, the wine list is good and the cassoulet (€17.50) and confit (€16.50) are simple and tender. However, with waiter call buttons, nautical servers' uniforms and Huey Lewis piped over the sound system, it all seems a bit gimmicky, like the dodgy booze cruises that plague the Thames with bad DJs and Bacardi Breezers. A nice change of pace, then, but not the place for an anniversary dinner. Alfresco dining weather permitting, cruises on Thursdays.

*Grand Canal, Mespil Road, Dublin 2.*
*087 7900077.*
*www.lapeniche.ie*

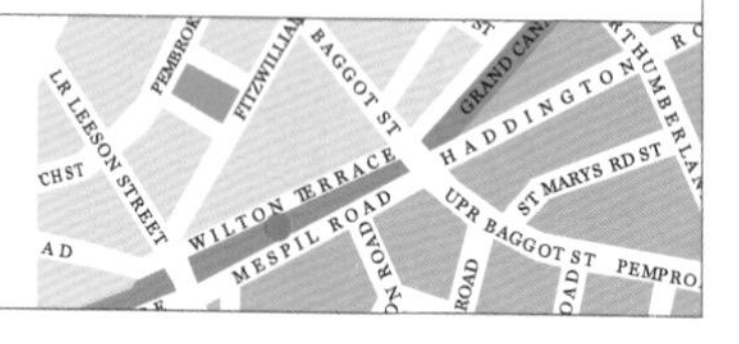

# PEARL BRASSERIE

*Little Gem*

It is among the most cherished myths of our time: expensive restaurants make lots of money. This is simply not true, as Ray Kroc – and a million other hamburger salesmen – will tell you. High-end places often struggle to survive, and it is particularly hard to thrive as a minnow in the shadow of Patrick Giblets. All of this makes the story of Kirsten Batt and Sebastian Masi remarkable. The young couple – he's French, she's Welsh – set up shop beside the Merrion, and they are still here eight years later. Masi's cooking is accomplished, the basement location is sweet and the service, led by Kirsten, is usually informed and enthusiastic. We have had several very fine meals here.

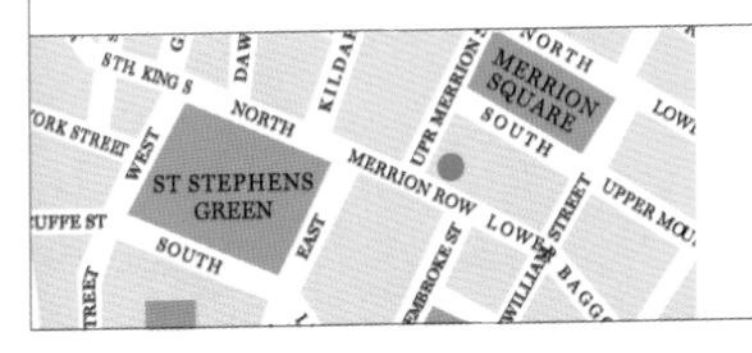


*20 Merrion Street Upper, Dublin 2.*
*661 3572.*
*www.pearl-brasserie.com*

# PEPLOE'S

*Posh Wine Bar*

Barry Canny is – as the name suggests – one of the shrewdest operators on Stephen's Green. He opened and sold Brownes, took the key staff and set up shop in a converted bank vault up the road. His basement homage to the Ivy is perhaps a tad OTT, but the food at this self-styled 'wine bistro' is not particularly expensive and the wine list is stunning. No-brainers on the short, simple lunch menu are the deep-fried brie in filo with pruneaux d'Agen (€7.95) and the cottage pie (€12.50). The atmosphere is warm and urbane. Quite a scene, too: bankers oil their clients, adworld bigwigs seduce their staff. Finally, be fussy enough about where they sit you. There are *several* bad tables.

*16 St Stephen's Green,*
*Dublin 2.*
*676 3144.*
*www.peploes.com*

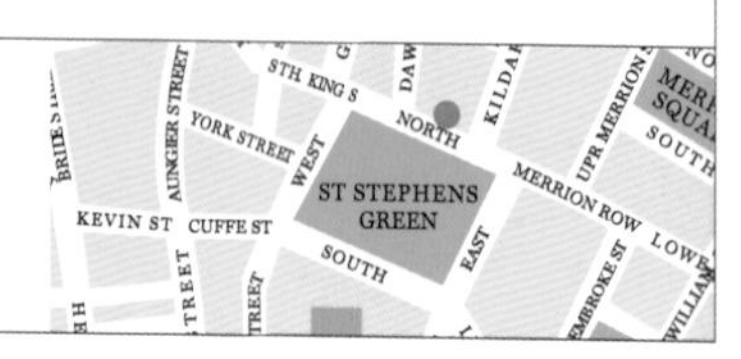

# PIZZA STOP

*Cheap Italian*

Unpretentious, friendly, welcoming. Three words that are rarely used to describe restaurants a week before Christmas. They can be applied to this family-run trattoria on Chatham Lane, even if the plastic tablecloths put the fear of God into granny. We start with the antipasto selection of cold cut meats and olives (€9.50). The olives are so-so, but the Parma ham is seriously delicious. (We've all been a victim of those salty strips of leather which are all too often served as Parma.) We follow with pizzas and a half bottle of the house red. Both fine. Tables are close together, so there is great earwigging potential if you are a budding social anthropologist/nosey parker.

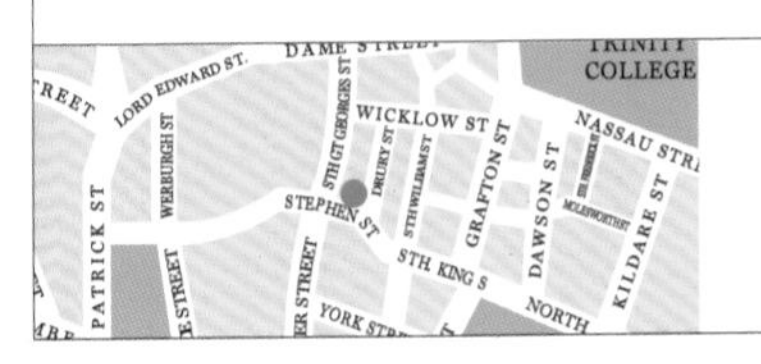


*6-10 Chatham Lane,*
*Dublin 2.*
*679 6712*

# THE PORT HOUSE

*Darkness*

Wow. It's dark in here. There's little you can do with such a small, cavernous brick chamber, but to Oliver Hughes' credit – you'll appreciate this once your eyes adjust – he didn't fight City Hall with tons of bright LEDs, opting instead for intimate nightlights and candles everywhere to create a Spanish bodega feel. Flattering light... great for dates! There are about 20 tapas dishes to try, divided into *frio* (cold), *caliente* (hot) and *pinchos*. Standout dishes are the *frango piri piri* (chargrilled chicken wings, €4.50) and *pulpo a la Gallega* (Gallixian octopus, €9). You'll have a wait for a table on Fridays and Saturdays, as they don't take bookings – put your name down and hop across to Grogan's for a swift half.

*64a South William Street, Dublin 2.*
*677 0298*

# POULOT'S

*Expensive French*

This elegant venue was, in a previous incarnation, Ernie's, one of Dublin's few good restaurants back in the days when Ireland had more in common with communist Poland than four shared letters. Secreted in a laneway behind Kiely's pub, it was a place in which the party *apparatchiks* dined their sub-rosa squeezes. We've been fans of Jean-Michel Poulot since his tenure at Halo, in its heyday the temple of tall, tortured food with Jean-Michel as high priest. Nowadays food has subsided to a lateral plane and M.Poulot does *bas-relief* in style. His empathy with fish, in particular, is total; on a recent visit we were enchanted by both the tuna and the John Dory. Bold wine list. Pricey.

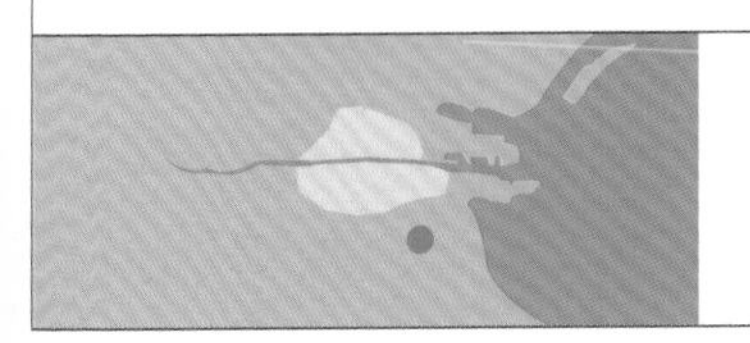

*Mulberry Garden,*
*Donnybrook, Dublin 4.*
*269 3300.*
*www.poulots.ie*

# IL PRIMO

*Reborn Italian*

Dieter Bergman has offloaded this little Italian to his manager and chef, John Farrell and Anita Thoma. The downstairs bar area – the best place to sit – has been redecorated, and the atmosphere now feels less intimidating. John has a nice word for all the women and they, in turn, have their eye on him. Anita's cooking also seems strangely liberated; we often complained that the portions were too small and the prices were too high. Today the highlights are a starter of pan-fried strips of marinated sirloin beef on a bed of rocket with Parmesan shavings (€9), a creamy smoked haddock risotto (€15) and a crab, leek and lemon lasagne (€18). In 1999 the same dish was £25.

*16 Montague Street,*
*Dublin 2.*
*478 3373.*
*www.ilprimo.ie*

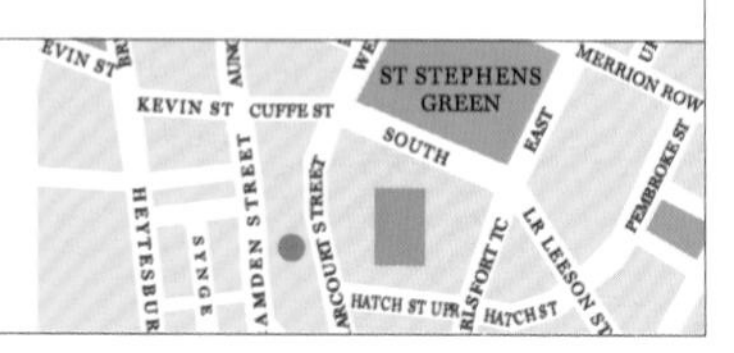

# THE PURTY KITCHEN

*Suburban Funhouse*

The owner of the Purty Kitchen, Conor Martin, trained at the Berkeley Court and the Merrion. Just as well. Once, he had to remove a senior minister from the premises – "and drive his car home with him in it. He was going around the tables whispering in the ears of customers and creating a very embarrassing situation for them." Such behaviour is, sadly, rare enough. A pub, restaurant and private members bar, the new-improved Purty Kitchen is a spirited venture. Service is okay, the decor is elegant and homely – old-fashioned meets colourful modernism – and the food isn't bad. Good seafood chowder (€4.95), fine big prawn cocktail, and tasty seafood specials.

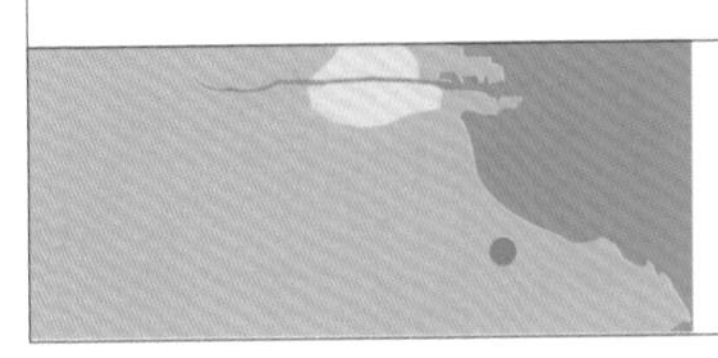

*Old Dun Laoghaire Road, Monkstown. 284 3576. www.purtykitchen.com/dunlaoghaire*

# QUEEN OF TARTS

*Adorable Café*

If the smell of homemade cookies, cakes and tarts brings back memories of better times, you'll love the Queen of Tarts. Run by two New York-trained sisters, Regina and Yvonne Fallon, this tiny café is a massive hit. The French-inspired decor is maximum-cosy. Read: little chair, little table, knees and elbows everywhere. Go for a savoury pie to start: we love the roast chicken and coriander tartlets (€7.95). The ultimate hang-over cure is just €6.75: bacon, egg, home-made potato cake, tomato, relish, toast and tea/coffee. Desserts are sublime: meringues, cookies and an apple crumble that will bring a tear to your eye. Try to get a window seat mid-morning with a paper. Bliss.

*4 Cork Hill, Dame Street, Dublin 2.*
*670 7499*

# RASAM

*Favourite Indian*

This place gets a lot of praise. Why? Nisheeth Tak is a charming maitre d', and his carefully sculpted dining room is a comfortable refuge. Note the dream-like palate of purples and creams, colourful pillows, feathers and genuine silver platters from Eastern palaces. Tak has cut the original capacity (150) in half to give regulars (which include Sinead O'Connor and Pat Kenny – not together, as far as we know) more room. The food is usually excellent. On our last visit, we had the sublime *varuval* lamb (€19.95): rich in colour and taste and partnered with a balanced combination of peppercorn, coriander and coconut milk. Delicious. One of the city's top Indian restaurants.

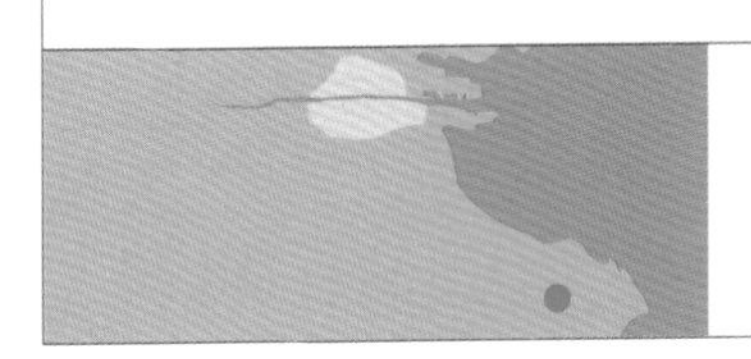

*18/19 Glasthule Road,*
*Dun Laoghaire.*
*230 0600.*
*www.rasam.ie*

# ROLY'S BISTRO

*A Classic*

Roly's has its detractors. We are not among them. The busiest restaurant in Dublin caters for suits and conference-goers escaping for lunch, rich locals and tourists. Head chef Paul Cartwright offers modern Irish fare in buzzy surroundings. Roly's is informal but classy, with an old-fashioned devil in the details – home-baked breads, crisp tablecloths. Start with the Caesar salad (€10.95) – this is what it's supposed to taste like. Then have Dublin Bay prawns, pan-fried with garlic, chili and ginger butter with wild rice (€33.95): one of the most expensive things on the menu, but a firm favourite. A four-course lunch menu costs just €20.95 and the best tables are 10 and 11.

*7 Ballsbridge Terrace,*
*Dublin 4.*
*668 2611.*
*www.rolysbistro.ie*

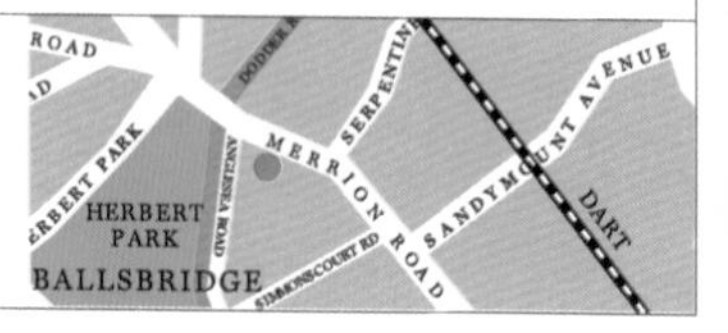

# SABA

*Asian Mischief*

Paul Cadden ran Diep Le Shaker before opening this ethnic winner in a room once occupied by the venerable Rajdoot Tandoori. The dining room, which has been opened up, now feels chic yet also more approachable. Older diners will not appreciate the bench seating that lines the windows – great for birthdays, stags and hens – but Cadden has cunningly divided up the space (ask for a banquette). The head chef, who worked for the King of Thailand, offers standard Thai and Vietnamese dishes alongside more esoteric fare. Try the duck spring roll (€7.35) or the sublime smoked trout *mieng kam* with ginger, shallots, lime and peanuts (€9.25). Pleasantly raucous atmosphere at the weekend.

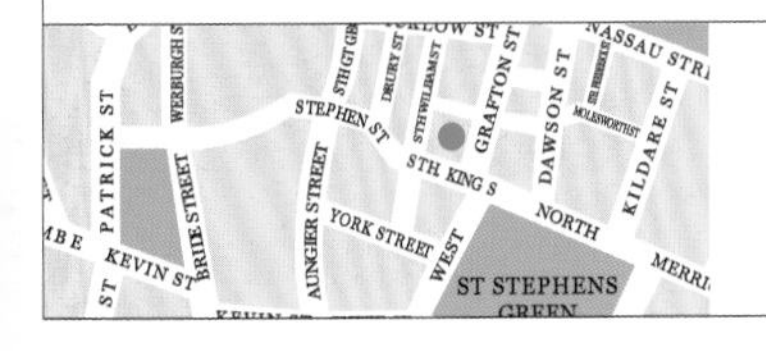


*26-28 Clarendon Street,*
*Dublin 2.*
*679 2000.*
*www.sabadublin.com*

# THE SADDLE ROOM

*New Side Door*

Bernard McNamara spent €100 million on restoring Dublin's most celebrated address. He has boldly re-imagined the Shelbourne for the 21st Century. The menu in the elegant new Saddle Room is full of staples – little room for invention on the part of chef John Mooney. A lobster seviche is the standout starter (€16), unless you want a plate of oysters. Entrées are excellent. Have anything from the grill, and if, like me, you enjoy a bit of Béarnaise, don't be afraid to ask for it. Twelve ounces of prime sirloin for €32 sounds reasonable in smart surroundings, though you will need to order sides. Have the potato gratin, the caramelised cauliflower and the onion rings. Watch your waist tomorrow.

*The Shelbourne,*
*27 St Stephen's Green,*
*Dublin 2.*
*663 4500*

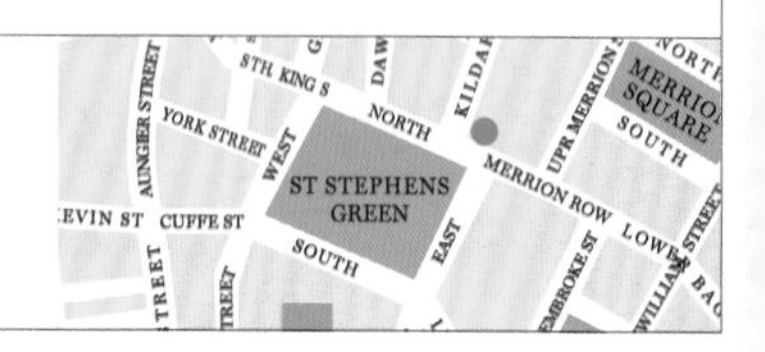

# SHANAHAN'S

*Class on the Green*

This legendary steakhouse is not cheap, but it's perfect for a special occasion. Come for elephantine portions of steak and seafood, served with great 'soul food' sides. Expect comfortable, spacious decor and excellent service. John Shanahan, an ebullient American of Irish descent, acquired the premises in 1998 with a view to creating the country's best steakhouse. There are plenty of meat and seafood options, but you simply have to go for beef, and while you're at it, a 24oz Bone-In Rib Eye. Order melt-in-the-mouth onion rings and creamed sweetcorn. Eat, sit back, relax – and head downstairs to the ritzy bar for a cocktail before bed. Or are you going to Lillie's?

*119 St Stephen's Green,*
*Dublin 2.*
*407 0939.*
*www.shanahans.ie*

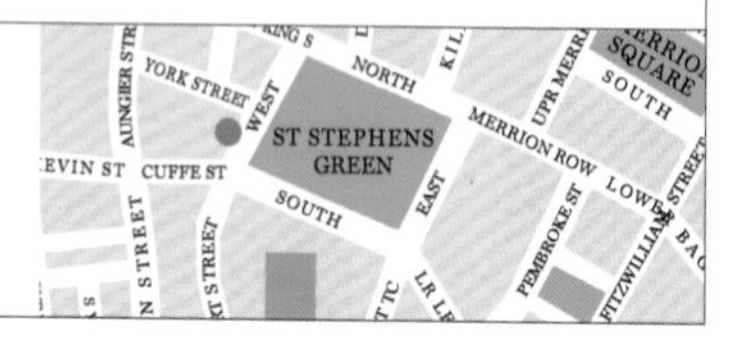

# SILK ROAD CAFÉ

*Eastern Lunches*

**Don't let** tourists be the only ones to enjoy this place. Located in the underrated Chester Beatty, the Silk Road offers a wide selection of Middle Eastern and Mediterranean dishes, prepared by Syrian, Palestinian and Lebanese chefs. We love the Jordanian *monsef* (layers of flat bread with lamb, rice, yoghurt and pine nuts) and Lebanese *kataif* – pancakes filled with nuts and coconut. Over half of the dishes are vegetarian, and everything is halal and kosher. All big, colourful, relatively cheap and very tasty. Don't forget to stock up on Turkish delight, sugared almonds and exotic teas and coffees on the way out. Nothing is particularly expensive, and it's all good.

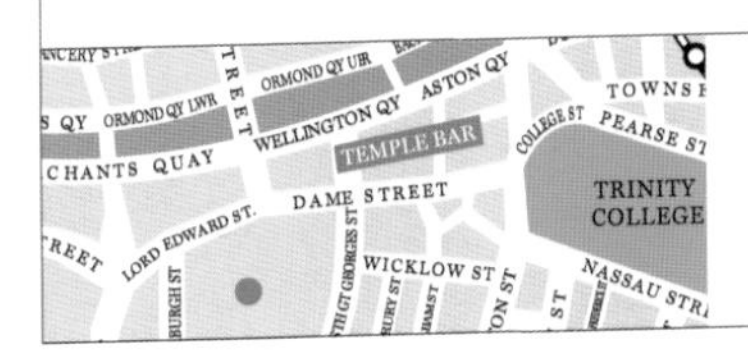


*Chester Beatty Library, Dublin Castle, Dublin 2, 407 0770. www.silkroadcafe.ie*

# SIMON'S PLACE

*Up the Revolution*

This busy little café on South Great George's Street is open for breakfast and lunch. Popular with students, buskers and couriers, it has a communal vibe that delicate suits may find a bit upsetting. The owner, Simon, does the washing up. His female staff remind us of Israeli soldiers – they're foreign, slightly intimidating and *very* attractive. The customers are a soulful bunch (yes, that *is* Camille O'Sullivan) and the food is hearty, simple and cheap, without being particularly ambitious or innovative. Believe it or not, the best thing on the menu is a prawn sandwich, which one might have with a cup of soup for just €7.40. *Prawn sandwich shocker in lefty café.* What is the world coming to?

*22 South Great George's Street, Dublin 2.*
*679 7821*

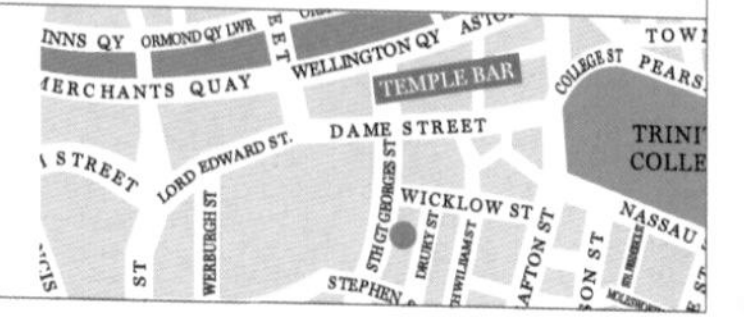

Santa Rita is
one of them.

Santa Rita

Memorable Every Time

www.santarita.com

Enjoy Santa Rita sensibly

# SOUTH

*Industrial Chic*

Suburbia now covers half the size of the greater Los Angeles area, yet we still talk about popping into town for dinner. How quaint. But lo, the new Dublin strides forth! Witness the arrival of Ronan Ryan's South Bar and Restaurant. Having lunch in an industrial estate has never been so chi-chi. Try the beer batter lemon sole or an 8oz beef burger, which comes at a price (€14.95) pleasing to the pocket of local residents with obligatory crippling mortgage. Chef Temple Garner's old favourites litter the dinner menu: we love the cannelloni al forno (€23.95), and a rib eye with smoked bacon, pearl onion jus and mash (€26.95). Great cocktail scene, cool dining room and good service. A winner.

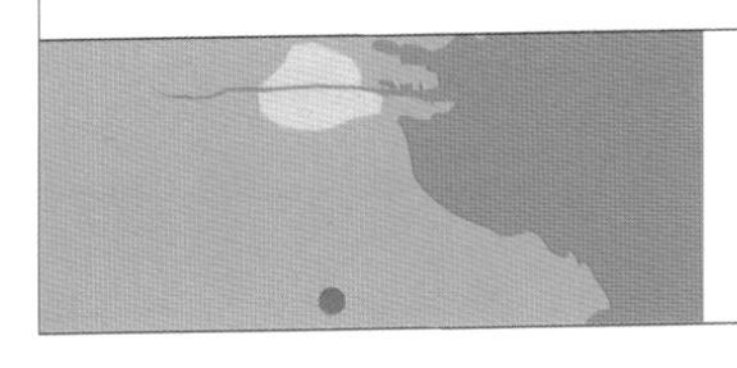

*Blackthorn Road, Sandyford, Dublin 18. 293 4050. www.southbarandrestaurant.com*

# THE SOUTH WILLIAM

*Funky Bar*

We like the South William. Troy Maguire and Conor Higgins (late of l'Gueuleton) have created a pie-only menu for the boozer of the moment. Get your gnashers around the duck confit and red cabbage or the beef shin and Guinness numbers (all €9). When the Romans first introduced pies to England they were referred to as 'coffins.' We can think of no finer resting place for a dead duck or the lower leg of a slaughtered cow than these short-crusted sarcophagi, replete with a 'D' or a 'B' as epitaph upon a glorious pastry headstone. The ultimate comfort food makes for the ultimate pub grub and there's no use dicking around with anything else – a pie and a pint will gladly suffice.

*52 South William Street,*
*Dublin 2.*
*672 5946.*
*www.southwilliam.ie*

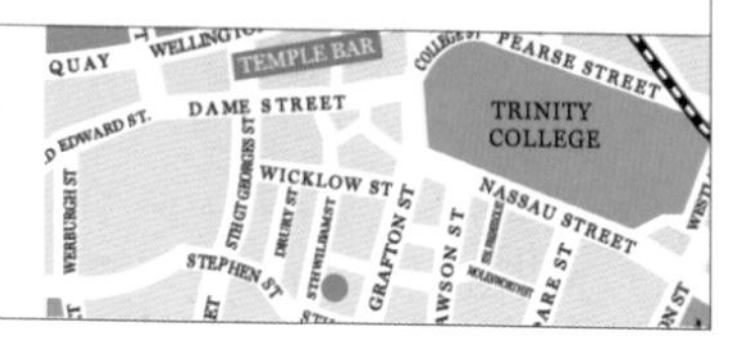

# STILL

*Meet Young Models*

The general manager of the Dylan says Still is the best restaurant in Dublin. Oh yeah? Like the rest of this funky boutique hotel, the dining room resembles a *Wallpaper* shoot in, say, 2002: grand piano, decadent chandeliers, sumptuous white palate. All *very* expensive. Models love it. Service is now – after hiccups – efficient. The food is 'experimental' Irish: we had oysters with tomato consommé and caviar (€18) to start – confusing, but tasty – and a fine roast beef fillet with wild mushroom ravioli (€38). It's easy to play it safe in Dublin, where even mediocre restaurants get a crowd at peak times (not for long!); this place doesn't play it safe. Not Dublin's best restaurant. But certainly not the worst.

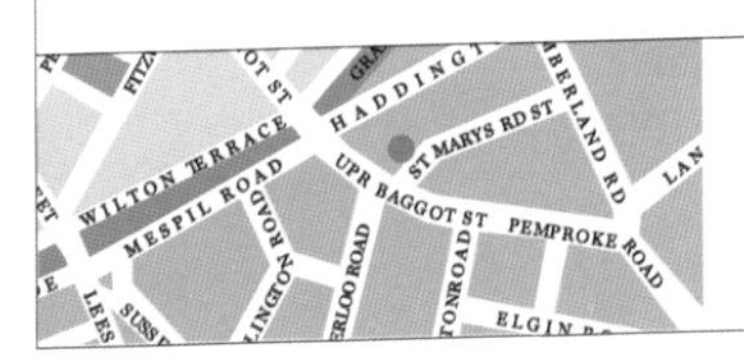


*Eastmoreland Place,*
*Dublin 4.*
*660 3000.*
*www.dylan.ie*

# STOOP YOUR HEAD

*Local Seafood*

This quaint pub is our favourite thing about the unremarkable seaside village of Skerries. Customers come from all over the county to indulge in Andy Davies' mainly seafood menu. The surroundings are simple and unpretentious, with chunky wood furniture and a blackboard menu announcing the specials. What better place to try a bowl of Dublin Bay prawns? Fried in garlic butter, fresh and delicious, they are €18.95. Sublime crab claws are the other reason to rave about this place. Indoors caters for 50, the outside dining area for 20 – great harbour views on a clear day. You may well have to wait for a table, but it's worth it: this little place is special.

*Harbour Road, Skerries,*
*County Dublin.*
*849 2085*

# THE TEA ROOM

*Rock Star Chic*

Haute cuisine at bistro prices. Try the two-course lunch (€26), guaranteed to have you in and out in 45 minutes, or have dinner before 8pm: three courses for €39. Expect mini tasteens of five starters to begin with – almost too pretty to eat – and a choice of daily specials. Your dad would complain about the portion sizes, but they're deceptive: this is good, thoughtful food, Irish with an international twist. Try the pan-fried monkfish in Parma ham. It's beautifully presented and served with flair. In fact, you'll be spoiled from start (a choice of eight homebaked breads) to finish (gourmet chocolates served with your coffee). And, yes, it's one of Dublin's most handsome dining rooms. Ask for table 40.

*The Clarence Hotel,*
*6-8 Wellington Quay,*
*Dublin 2. 407 0800.*
*www.theclarence.ie*

# THORNTON'S

*Peerless Cooking*

The most talented chef this country has ever produced is the owner of a restaurant that few people bother to support. That is a telling indictment of the Irish; for all our talk of culinary revolutions and cappuccino culture, we don't really give a damn about good cooking. If we did, Thornton's would be packed every day (they don't even open for lunch). Thornton knows this, and in private he is inclined to admit it. I once asked him where he would recommend eating in Dublin. "At home," he replied. The Tipperary man is difficult to work with, and he couldn't be bothered to work the system. But his determination to produce eye-popping food in a city of blindness is admirable.

*The Fitzwilliam Hotel,*
*128 St Stephen's Green,*
*Dublin 2. 478 7000.*
*www.fitzwilliamhotel.*

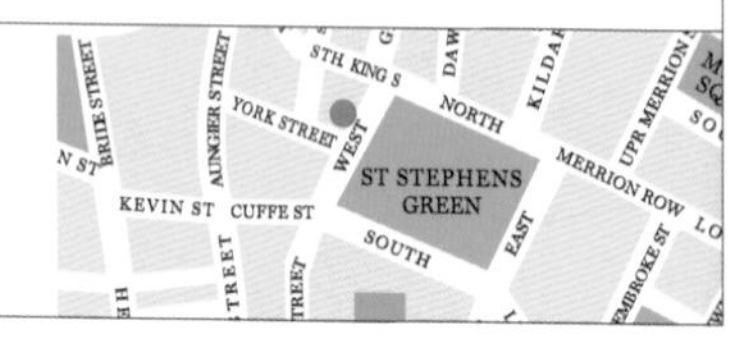

# TOWN BAR & GRILL

*Basement Style*

Temple Garner, the talented ex-Il Primo, ex-Mermaid chef, is the brains behind this trattoria around the corner from the Shelbourne. It's named after NYC's Old Town Bar, a speakeasy during Prohibition times. But the similarities end with the name: the New York bar is mahogany, mobsters and burgers; its Kildare Street protégé is brick and white tableclothes, celebrities (Mary Harney! Twink!) and modern Italian cooking. Try the antipasti plate for starters (€10.95). Grilled John Dory comes with celestial Italian winter sprouting broccoli and lemon caper butter. Overcrowded, violently noisy, with triumphant food: Town Bar & Grill is a spectacular success – and it's *not* particularly expensive.

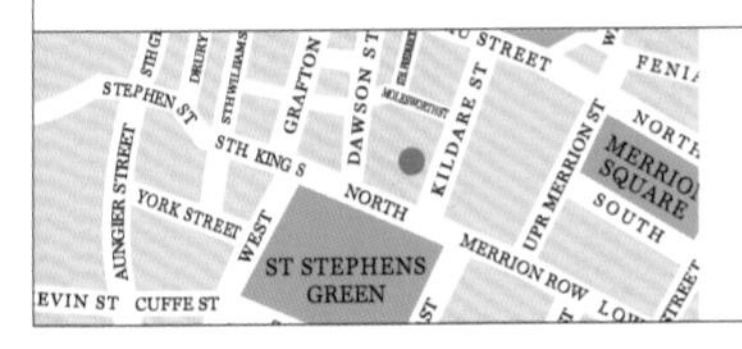


*21 Kildare Street, Dublin 2. 662 4724. www.townbarandgrill.com*

# TROCADERO

*Theatrical Legend*

Writing in *The Dubliner*, Helen Lucy Burke gave the Troc a pasting in 2007. Nothing about HLB's experience surprised me, although I have a different view of this luvvie legend. For me, the Troc is like a rich old friend who is always throwing her house open to thirsty strangers from worlds more tropical than my own. I love the air of mischief that descends on the bar around midnight, and I think it's sweet that the cannelloni has been made by Liz, Robert Doggett's sister, for the last 16 years. Robert is, of course, the star attraction here: a maitre d' with all the charisma of an old-school matinée idol, in a restaurant for part-time celebrities and full time-dreamers. Much craic.

*3 St Andrew's Street, Dublin 2. 677 5545. www.trocadero.ie*

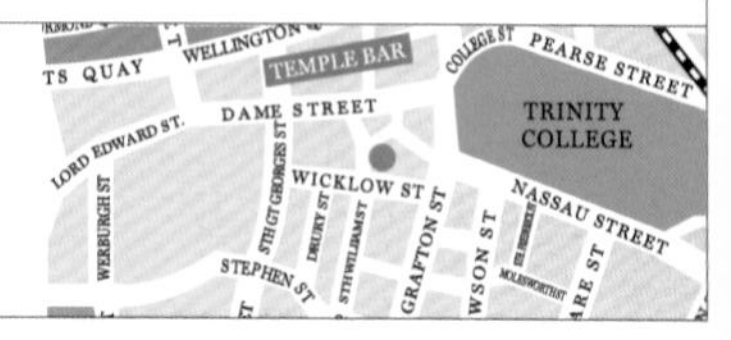

# UKIYO

*More than Karaoke*

We're still going on about this Japanese joint on Exchequer Street. You've heard it all before: the karaoke booths, the cute waitresses... did you know they've started doing brunch? It's an interesting alternative to eggs Benedict in Odessa. Smiling proprietor Duncan Maguire is still there most days. We arrived at brunch o'clock and blagged the only terrace table. The sun was shining, it was summer in Dublin (for half an hour) and all felt right in the world. We had a platter of mackerel marinated in lemon and ginger, with a pristine side salad, fried egg and rice and a damn fine Bloody Mary. Uki-Yo is principally renowned as a posh karaoke joint. It deserves a better rep.

*7/9 Exchequer Street,*
*Dublin 2. 633 4071.*
*www.ukiyobar.com*

# THE UNICORN

*Tiger HQ*

The Unicorn defines this era in the same way that Dobbins is synonymous with the early-1990s, or Whites on the Green was an icon of the late-1980s. But it's older than all of them, and it still unites generations in search of tipples/people-watching/something to do on a Friday afternoon. The Italian-Irish cooking was never the main attraction, although there is nothing wrong with the generous antipasti or a bowl of fresh prawns. Service is excellent, led by Giorgio Casari and his wife Noirin; they are genuinely charming people. Not cheap, and lunch is a lot more fun than dinner. But for sheer entertainment value – the restaurant as theatre – there is nowhere quite like it.

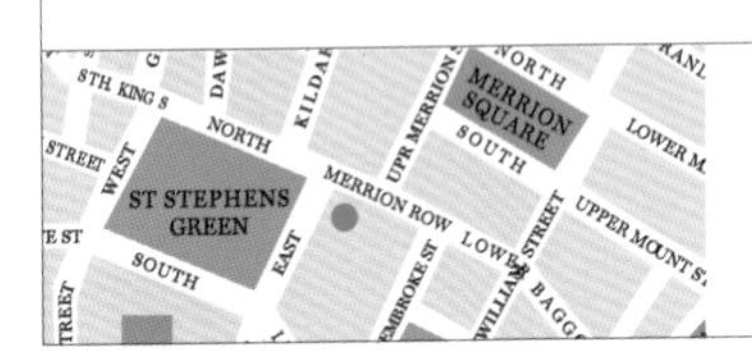


*12b Merrion Court, Merrion Row, Dublin 2. 676 2182. www. unicornrestaurant.com*

# VENU

*French Bunker*

Charlie Guilbaud opened this bistro-in-a-basement at the tender age of 27. It's a large, expensively-decorated venture. Unfortunately, the subterranean interior just doesn't feel cosy or lovable. We've moaned about this repeatedly, although papa's prominence in the business ensures that such gripes are rarely heard outside *The Dubliner*. "It seems set to become one of the country's most fashionable restaurants," gushed Tom Doorley. That was in 2006. Venu may yet become the most fashionable restaurant in Ireland – and the cooking is good solid bistro fare at decent prices – but we remain ambiguous about the venue. Mind you, the cocktails are fantastic.

*Anne's Lane, off South Anne's Street, Dublin 2. 670 6755. www.venu.ie*

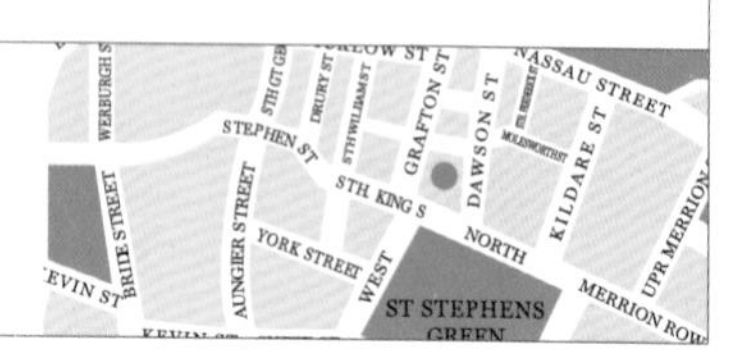

# VERMILION

*Indian Fusion*

If there were awards for marketing restaurants, Gerry Kochanski would win them every year. Gerry always mounts a campaign to win our People's Choice award, and Vermilion's high ranking is a testament to the loyalty of his customers. The restaurant itself is above a pub in Terenure. When it opened a few years back, critics gushed about the Indian-fusion cooking. The dining room still feels swankier than your average Indian, and the toilets are particularly impressive. We hear mixed reports about the food, but Kochanski could well moan about how representative our own sample is... statistics, eh? Not, then, Dublin's *best* Indian, but a popular choice nonetheless.

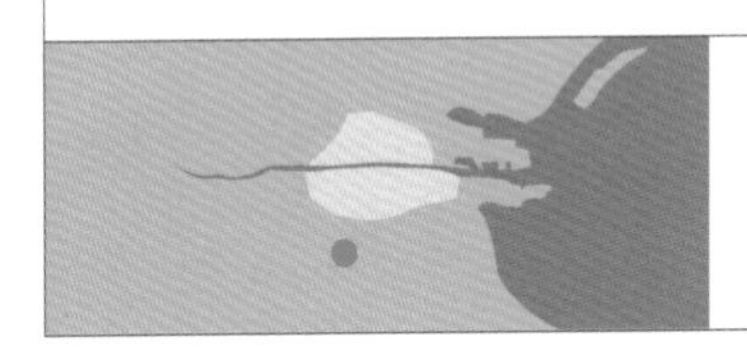

*94-96 Terenure Road North, Dublin 6W.*
*499 1400.*
*www.vermilion.ie*

# WAGAMAMA

*Cheap Fusion*

Wagamama is cheap. Don't expect an atmosphere of refined and exquisite hospitality, *Tea House of the August Moon* style: there are no bowing, simpering geishas and there are no chair-backs. And if you are trying to communicate carnal endearments, you do it at the full belt of your lungs. But this is also a phat spot, with helpful staff and tasty food. Try chilli beef ramen (€15.75), or have a splendid vegetarian wok-cooked dish called *yasai itame*: tofu, red peppers, sweet potato, butternut squash, courgettes, mange tout peas and mushrooms in a lightly spiced lemongrass and coconut sauce, with steamed Japanese style rice (€11.25). Great juices. The puddings are wholly unremarkable: avoid.

*South King Street,*
*Dublin 2.*
*478 2152.*
*www.wagamama.ie*

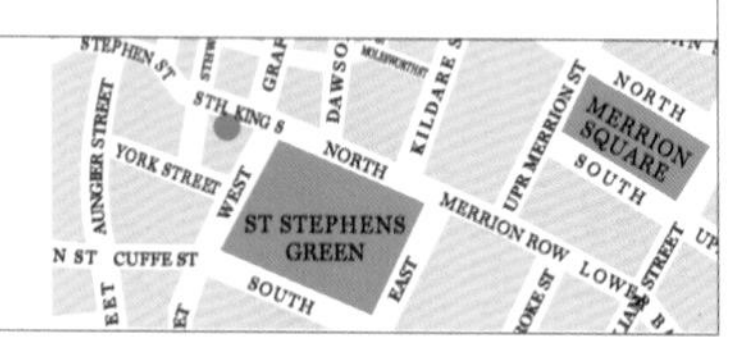

# THE WINDING STAIR

*HiCo Dream*

The Winding Stair was the most acclaimed opening of 2006 – yes, that *was* Ralph Fiennes – but, unusually for a comet, it still burns bright. It stands atop a wonderful odd bookshop, with lovely views along the Liffey. It's a full-on HiCo dream: traditional Irish food and an old-school vibe, but with a wine list as long as your arm and *macchiati* to follow. All ingredients are carefully sourced and many are organic. Split the Irish charcuterie board with homemade breads, pickles and relish (€12.50) to start, followed by Irish bacon collar with cabbage and parsley sauce (€19.50). They even serve a wide selection of micro-brews. (The dining room is small. Book well in advance.)

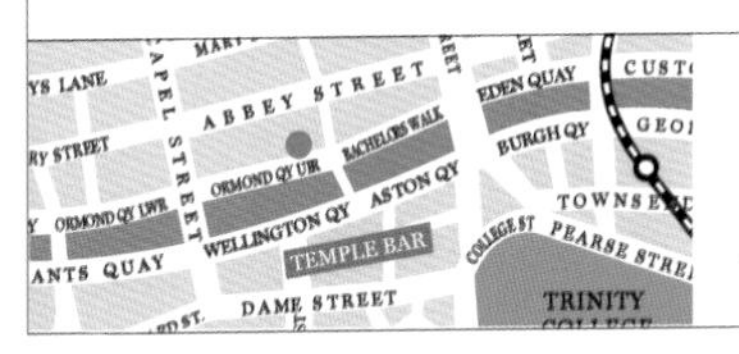


*40 Ormond Quay,*
*Dublin 1.*
*872 7320.*
*www.winding-stair.com*

# WHAT DO YOU WANT TO EAT?

## CHEAP & CHEERFUL



## IRISH



## ASIAN



## ITALIAN



## FRENCH

## MODERN EUROPEAN



## SEAFOOD



## POSH



## VEGETARIAN



## WORLD

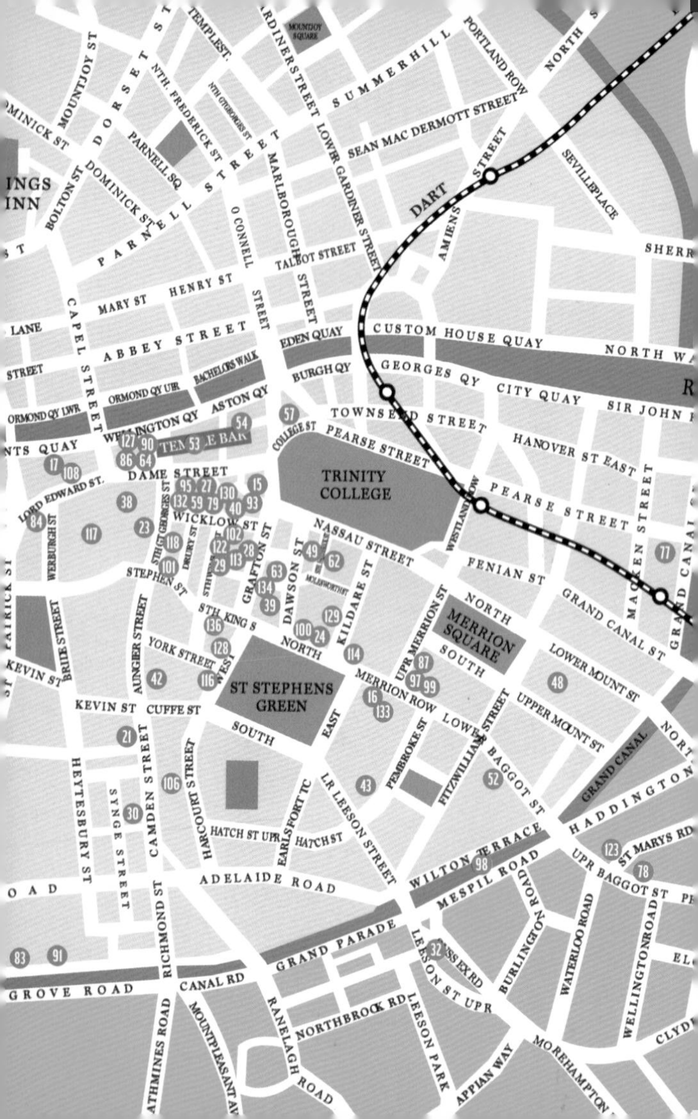

MOUNTJOY SQUARE
TEMPLE ST.
GARDINER STREET
SUMMERHILL
PORTLAND ROW
NORTH
MOUNTJOY ST
DORSET ST
NTH. FREDERICK ST
NTH GT GEORGES ST
SEAN MAC DERMOTT STREET
DOMINICK ST
PARNELL SQ
PARNELL STREET
MARLBOROUGH STREET
LOWER GARDINER STREET
AMIENS STREET
SEVILLE PLACE
KINGS INN
BOLTON ST
DOMINICK ST
DART
O CONNELL STREET
TALBOT STREET
SHERR
HENRY ST
MARY ST
CAPEL STREET
LANE
ABBEY STREET
EDEN QUAY
CUSTOM HOUSE QUAY
NORTH WA
STREET
BACHELORS WALK
BURGH QY
GEORGES QY
CITY QUAY
ORMOND QY UPR
ASTON QY
ORMOND QY LWR
WELLINGTON QY
TEMPLE BAR
COLLEGE ST
TOWNSEND STREET
SIR JOHN R
PEARSE STREET
HANOVER ST EAST
NTS QUAY
DAME STREET
TRINITY COLLEGE
LORD EDWARD ST.
WICKLOW ST
WESTLAND ROW
PEARSE STREET
NASSAU STREET
WERBURGH ST
STH GT GEORGES ST
DRURY ST
GRAFTON ST
DAWSON ST
KILDARE ST
FENIAN ST
MACKEN STREET
GRAND CANAL ST
STEPHEN ST
MOLESWORTH ST
NORTH
MERRION SQUARE
STH KING S
UPR MERRION ST
SOUTH
LOWER MOUNT ST
BRIDE STREET
AUNGIER STREET
YORK STREET
WEST
NORTH
KEVIN ST
ST STEPHENS GREEN
MERRION ROW
UPPER MOUNT ST
KEVIN ST
CUFFE ST
EAST
LOWER
FITZWILLIAM STREET
SOUTH
PEMBROKE ST
BAGGOT ST
GRAND CANAL
HEYTESBURY ST
SYNGE STREET
CAMDEN STREET
HARCOURT STREET
EARLSFORT TC
LR LEESON STREET
HADDINGTON
HATCH ST UPR
HATCH ST
WILTON TERRACE
ST MARYS RD
UPR BAGGOT ST
ADELAIDE ROAD
MESPIL ROAD
ROAD
RICHMOND ST
GRAND PARADE
LEESON ST UPR
SUSSEX RD
BURLINGTON ROAD
WATERLOO ROAD
WELLINGTON ROAD
GROVE ROAD
CANAL RD
NORTHBROOK RD
LEESON PARK
CLYDE
RATHMINES ROAD
MOUNTPLEASANT AV
RANELAGH ROAD
APPIAN WAY
MOREHAMPTON

# SOUTH CITY

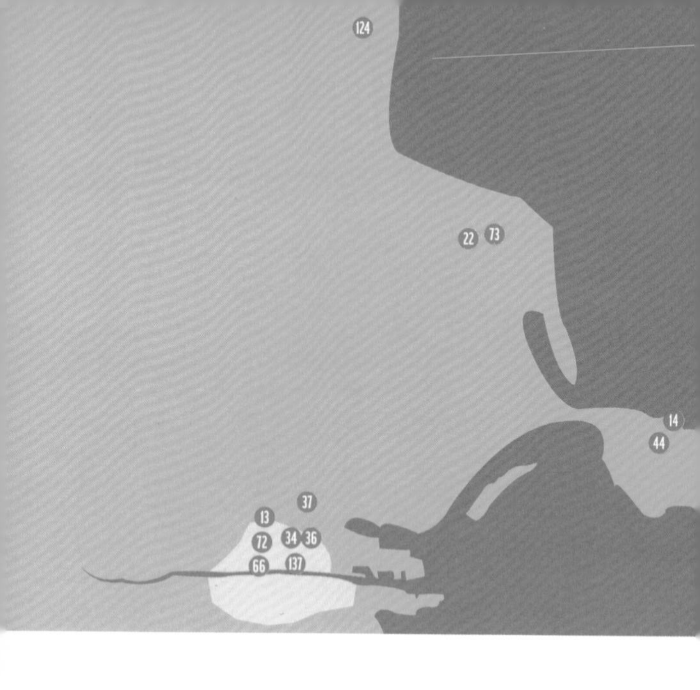


# NORTH CITY

# NEW ENTRIES...

# ...NEW EXITS

101 Talbot
Amnesty Café
Aya
Caife Una
Chatham Brasserie
China House
China-Sichuan
Cilantro
Cooper's
Frank's
Good World
Er Buchetto
Hanley at the Bar
Han Yang
Harry's
Honest to Goodness
Indian Summer
Kingfisher
Mackerel
La Mère Zou
Michael's
Il Posto
The Queens
Radha Govinda's
Rhodes D7
Siam Thai
Soup Dragon
Tonic

*Down...but not out.*

# SOUTH DUBLIN

# ACKNOWLEDGEMENTS

*The Dubliner* magazine has a panel of reviewers who contribute to the restaurant pages and this guide. The panel includes Helen Lucy Burke, Eoin Higgins, Ernie Whalley, Richard Lubell, Derek Owens, Marc Doyle, Emily Hourican, Ingmar Kiang, Helen O'Rourke, Paul Trainer and Eamon McLoughlin.

The editor wishes to acknowledge the support of Terry Pennington, Julia Kennedy and their colleagues at Gilbeys of Ireland, the distributors of Santa Rita wines in Ireland.

The staff of *The Dubliner*, in particular Art Director Simon O'Connor, Deputy Editor Nicola Reddy and Publishing Manager Paul Trainer, all contribute to the success of this book. This year, Ciara Hughes, Briana Komar, Shane O'Reilly, Christine Donaldson and Rachel Faulkner all assisted in the production of the book. The photography is by Klaudyna Karczewska. The book was proof read by, Daniel Philbin-Bowman and Catriona Gray.

---

TREVOR WHITE was educated at Sandford Park, St Columba's and Trinity College, before stints in London, Prague, New York and Bermuda. He became Features Editor of *Food and Wine* in 1997. Today White is the editor of *The Dubliner* magazine. His book, *Kitchen Con: Writing on the Restaurant Racket*, was published in 2006. This is the sixth edition of *The Dubliner 100 Best Restaurants*. The first edition of *The Dubliner 100 Best Bars* was published in 2007.

*Town Bar & Grill*